Jenny Herrick

GREATER
THAN RICHES

Daily
Readings
to Enrich
Your Walk
with God

John White

INTERVARSITY PRESS
DOWNERS GROVE, ILLINOIS 60515

InterVarsity Press is the book-publishing division of InterVarsity Christian Fellowship, a student movement active on campus at hundreds of universities, colleges and schools of nursing in the United States of America, and a member movement of the International Fellowship of Evangelical Students. For information about local and regional activities, write Public Relations Dept., InterVarsity Christian Fellowship, 6400 Schroeder Rd., P.O. Box 7895, Madison, WI 53707-7895.

All Scripture quotations, unless otherwise indicated, are taken from the HOLY BIBLE, NEW INTERNATIONAL VERSION. Copyright © 1973, 1978, 1984 International Bible Society. Used by permission of Zondervan Publishing House. All rights reserved.

Cover illustration: SuperStock, Inc.

ISBN 0-8308-1314-4

Printed in the United States of America ∞

Library of Congress Cataloging-in-Publication Data
White, John, 1924 Mar. 5-
    Greater than riches: daily readings to enrich your walk with
    God/John White.
       p.   cm.
     ISBN 0-8308-1314-4
     1. Devotional exercises. I. Title.
BV4832.2.W5117 1991
242'.2—dc20   92-1271
                                     CIP

15	14	13	12	11	10	9	8	7	6	5	4	3	2
03	02	01	00	99	98	97	96	95	94	93	92		

Preface

God wants to meet with you. He wants to have fellowship with you. In fact, he wants this so much that he is pursuing you. He does not do so because he needs you but because you need him. His is the tenderness of a mother over a fretful infant. He is there. He is speaking. And you may sit in quietness to drink in his beauty, trembling with joy.

It may take you time to learn the confidence of going into his presence. Many books have been written on techniques for this. But I believe only two things are necessary.

First, you must recognize that the Holy Spirit has already become your teacher. Don't ask *how* you can best cooperate with him. The teaching and training is *his* job, and in his own way and time he will teach you. Second, let the truth of what I have already said sink into the quietness of your heart—God desires you more than you desire him.

It is the purpose of this book to provide one means by which you may meet with God. The format is simple—a verse of Scripture, a brief thought, a concluding prayer. The formula is not magical. It does not guarantee a spiritual experience. But God may choose to use these words in your life for his glory.

These readings are selected from a dozen of my other books. Do not feel bound to read them daily; dip into them as best suits you. Do not be limited by my brief prayers; use them as a springboard for your own.

May the Lord use these readings to remind you of his truth and his mighty love, and may he lead you deeper into the life that is greater than riches.

John White

MONTH ONE

ONE. Greater Than Riches ◊

My ears had heard of you but now my eyes have seen you.
JOB 42:5

W e think of the book of Job as a story of suffering. But it is more. Job was a good man who honored God and was rewarded by God. Yet in response to Satan's cynicism about Job, God allows Satan to inflict whatever pain he wishes, provided only that Job's life be spared. As a result a series of catastrophes overwhelms Job. He loses his fortune, his children, his health and even the respect and support of his wife.

Wretched, in pain and profoundly depressed, he refuses either to despair or to curse God and die. His friends exhort him to recognize that his difficulties are the result of his sin. God is never to blame, they say. Therefore the blame must be Job's. Job maintains that if he could talk to God, then God would confirm that Job has done nothing wrong.

But then God comes.

God reminds Job that Job didn't create the earth or the seas or the heavens. God is not reacting to Job out of pride nor is his speech from the whirlwind a haughty putdown. God's correction is designed to restore Job's perspective, indeed to improve it. And it is plain that Job retains God's warm approval. Job is vindicated not by his righteousness but by God's mercy while his friends are condemned.

The fact that Job has twice as much property and twice as many children by the end of the story may mean little to us. We are inclined to be supercilious about stories which end, "And they all lived happily ever after." Yet in an age when such things (prosperity, children) were seen as signs of divine approval, they were meant to tell us that pain is not necessarily punishment. Those whom God loves may indeed undergo trials which need not imply sin or divine wrath.

The problem of suffering remains incompletely solved in the book, but for Job it no longer existed. It was not just that his fortunes were restored. Something greater than earthly riches had come into his life, the richness a person knows when he or she treasures the majesty and glory of God. Such riches breed deep contentment. Job eventually died "old and full of years."

"Now my eyes have seen you." Perhaps if you begin to catch even a vicarious glimpse of awesomeness, you may begin to understand its relevance. It is immaterial whether you ever tangle with a whirlwind. What matters is that God should receive from you the worship that such a God merits.

Mighty God, I do worship you. You are very God of very God. Every breath that fills my lungs comes from you. No one else is worthy to rule the universe. Even in the midst of suffering I remember that your merciful presence and work are greater than riches to me. Praise to you, Lord. Amen.

TWO. Recommitment ◊

Suppose a king is about to go to war against another king. Will he not first sit down and consider whether he is able with ten thousand men to oppose the one coming against him with twenty thousand?

LUKE 14:31

I retired because the demands of writing books began to compete with the psychiatric and academic sides of my life, and I had to choose one or the other. After praying about the matter for a year or two, my wife, Lorrie, and I decided I should opt for writing. So we bought a fairly isolated condominium on the shore of a large lake that had several thousand islands. There I could write in solitude.

It was gorgeous. Winter in the country is spectacular, and all necessary snow clearing was done for us. We had central heating for warmth and even a plentiful supply of firewood which was cut and stacked for us. As for the other seasons, each had its special joy. For me the year or so we spent by the lake was a time of healing. I would walk through the woods and let their peace soak into me. And, of course,

I would write and study and pray.

But gradually my paradise began to seem less attractive. Something was missing. We were active in Christian work; my writing seemed to be owned by God. Yet I could not shake the feeling that we were in a sort of backwater. I began to ask God to take me to the battlefront. I wanted to be where he himself was most in evidence.

One day Lorrie said to me, "You know, I've been praying for some time about something. I'm not happy here, John."

"I know it's rough. You're a people person and we're a bit cut off."

"But it's more than that. I feel so useless. *I want to be where the battle is.*"

My remorse suddenly turned to joy. "You too? I've been praying that for months. I want to die with my boots on."

So we began to pray together for an assignment at the front line of the battle—wherever that be. We did not fully realize it, but we were recommitting ourselves to God. For commitment is never a static thing. From time to time we need a new vision and a renewal of our vows, a new decision to follow fully, to the death if need be.

Father, I am grateful that your assignments are good ones for me and that following you is always an adventure. Help me to be content when you say stay and ready when you say go. Amen.

THREE. In Training ◊

Everyone who competes in the games goes into strict training.
1 CORINTHIANS 9:25

I learned to swim by having a beautiful experience. At the shallow end of the pool I saw a coin wavering on the tile floor. I was chest-deep in water. Grabbing the coin meant immersing my whole body in water. Under the water I couldn't see too well, but after a few tries I was successful.

But I picked up something more valuable than a coin. I found I couldn't keep my feet on the bottom. Each time I was getting low enough to grope, my feet would lose touch with the floor and start to rise. At first this was disconcerting. But suddenly it dawned on me that *I had begun to float.* Once I could maintain a little tranquility I found my face was still under the water, but the back of my head and my shoulders were on the surface. My body was hanging in watery space, freed from the bonds of gravity like that of an astronaut. It was a glorious moment. That morning I swam from one side of the pool to the other without touching the bottom once.

My experience was valid. I really did float. My floating was not imaginary. I had learned to trust the water to uphold me. My experience was also transforming. I entered the pool as a defeated struggler. I left it a swimmer.

But my experience, while making me a real swimmer, did not make me a good swimmer. Rigid training and hard practice were needed. I even had moments of further illumination in swimming, breakthroughs in which I experienced a new freedom in the water. Most of them came *during the process of training.* Without the training none of them would have given me my present ability in the water.

What holds true for swimmers and swimming also holds true for Christians and godly living. Biblical knowledge and spiritual breakthroughs are not enough. Godliness also demands training.

Thank you, Lord, for the glorious moments you have given from time to time in my walk with you. I dare not ask for more of them. Instead, I ask that you will train me to walk in obedience and thereby learn godliness. Amen.

FOUR. The Enraged Jesus ◊

So he made a whip out of cords, and drove all from the temple area, both sheep and cattle; he scattered the coins of the money changers and overturned their tables.

JOHN 2:15

H e made the whip himself. Therefore his act of enraged violence was premeditated, not an impulsive outburst. At what was the Son of God enraged?

It is an important question. In a life marked by gentleness and compassion this incident alone sees Jesus as a man of violence. Friends and foes alike were awed and bewildered. His previous verbal outbursts against the Pharisees were hardly gentle. But only on this occasion did he resort to violence.

What was it about the traffic in coins and animals that offended him so deeply? "A house of prayer" he had called it, not a place of teaching nor yet a place of sacrifice. (He himself was to be the sacrifice.) What was in his mind?

The priests' idea of reverence was perilously close to respect for themselves, for their religious system and all they in the pomp of their positions thought they stood for. They would have been shocked had you told them they no longer stood for Yahweh and his name. But you would have been telling the truth. They were guilty of idolatry. The dignity of the buildings was what mattered to them.

A place of prayer. In the purposes of God, the Temple was to be a place in which all nations might have access to him. In their spiritual declension the Pharisees and Sadducees had lost true reverence for God.

And though it hurts me deeply to say it, many churches today seem to have no reverence for him. Arrogantly, we worship our own institutions, our buildings, our programs. It is a sick and devilish worship for these things to reflect our glory, beaming our egocentric worship back upon ourselves to exalt us in the eyes of the world and of our religious competitors. We have become gods in our idolatrous religious empires.

Do we share the outlook of the priests rather than that of Jesus? What do we say when small children run laughing and chasing inside our church buildings? Do we say, "Hush! This is God's house!" If so we teach them a lie. God does not dwell in buildings of cement and steel any more than in pseudo-Gothic showpieces. His people are his dwelling place.

Christ, you lashed out against idolatry, against self-worship. I want to look beyond human structures, and beyond my own needs, to worship with pure heart and motives. Forgive me and help me, I pray. Amen.

FIVE. Collaborating with God ◊

I waited patiently for the LORD; he turned to me and heard my cry.
PSALM 40:1

M any years ago, during my student days, I came across a booklet entitled *Prayer: Focused and Fighting* by G. H. Lang. The author points out that intercessory prayer begins with God. God does not call on us to decide on the battle strategy and then to ask his help in carrying out our plans. Rather we are to ask him what *his* plans are. To do so we are to wait on God so that he can reveal his mind to us.

According to Lang this greatly simplifies prayer. We will find that just as battles often hinge on one focal point, so a simple request may be the key to resolving vast, complex issues. In place of a list of requests we may need to make only one—provided we see the battle as God sees it.

I was impressed enough to put Lang's advice rigorously into practice. I knew that my subjective impressions about what God said might not always be reliable. So I purchased a notebook and recorded my traffic with God in prayer.

My responsibilities with Inter-Varsity had increased and were now on a national scale. Deliberately I spent time waiting in God's presence as I brought one situation after another before him. I would not intercede at once but would ask God how he wanted me to pray. I would then pray according to what I felt was his leading. I would carefully record what I had prayed, the date on which I had prayed, the degree of certainty I had felt about his will and biblical evidence supporting my certainty. Then I would leave a space in which to record the results of my prayer.

Often I would be astounded by the accuracy and effectiveness of such requests.

On one occasion a serious situation was developing because one influential leader was leading large numbers of groups in a dangerous direction. The issue was to come to a head at a certain meeting, a meeting I could not possibly attend. How ought I pray? What ought I to do?

As I waited on God it seemed he was saying, "Pray that he will repent and admit his error at that meeting."

"But Lord, he's not the kind of man who would do that!"

"Pray that he will repent!"

"But Lord . . ."

"Pray that he will repent!"

I did. And a week later the astonishing news of his profound change of heart reached me. The crisis was over. The tragedy I dreaded never took place. It was not my powerful praying that had changed matters but the fact that I was collaborating with God's plans.

I must not pretend I was always right. At other times I would be hopelessly mistaken about the Spirit's direction. But if subsequent events proved me wrong, I could then go back to God and ask him why I had been mistaken. Soon it would become plain to me. Sometimes my pride or my own desires or prejudices had misled me. At other times I had overlooked an important biblical principle, for the Spirit's direction never violates revealed laws.

Slowly I became better at distinguishing the voice of God from the voices of my twisted desires. Off and on I have all my life continued to follow this practice, filling notebooks as I slowly learn to wait on God.

Teach me to wait quietly so I can hear your voice, Lord. Then I can pray confidently as you direct me. Amen.

SIX. The Real War ◊

For our struggle is . . . against the powers of this dark world and against the spiritual forces of evil in the heavenly realms.
EPHESIANS 6:12

From a safe distance of several hundred years or several thousand miles, revival clearly looks invigorating. What could be more glorious than a mighty work of God in our midst, renewing thousands and converting tens of thousands.

But when we actually look at a revival (through either close historical study or firsthand investigation) we find things not nearly so clear as we imagined. We find sin and infighting and doctrinal error. And if we find ourselves in the midst of revival, rather than being invigorated we may be filled with skepticism, disgust, anger or even fear. Why does our expectation not match the reality? Why is revival sometimes so messy?

One reason is that *revival is war,* and war is never tidy. It is an intensifying of the age-old conflict between Christ and the powers of darkness. But we may ask: Didn't Christ already win the victory? Can war in the spiritual realm have any meaning now that Christ has forever defeated the powers of darkness? Isn't the war over? And isn't the victory won primarily in the sphere of the lives of Christian believers?

Oscar Cullman tries to explain the paradox in terms of the Second World War. He sees the Normandy landings as a sort of equivalent to Calvary, in the sense that the world knew, when the Allies had landed successfully in Normandy, that the war was at an end—finished. The Allies had won. But the German High Command refused to accept reality and in their psychotic denial fought on. Indeed the bloodiest fighting of the war followed.

Hell's powers are equally insane. Doomed and hopeless, they fight on in spite of Calvary. Our own battle against them is real. We do not beat the air. We wrestle against principalities and powers, while an angelic host fights alongside us. From time to time cosmic mopping-up operations achieve other breakthroughs, what we call revival occurs and the invisible side of the picture seems for a time to become more apparent.

Jesus, free me from naive preconceptions about revival, so that I may not shrink from your working but may joyfully participate even when things are untidy. Amen.

SEVEN. Sin and Physical Disease ◊

Anyone who eats and drinks [the bread and the cup] without recognizing the body of the Lord eats and drinks judgment on himself. That is why many among you are weak and sick, and a number of you have fallen asleep.
1 CORINTHIANS 11:29-30

There are connections between sin and sickness. Sin gives rise to disease in two ways: directly and indirectly. All diseases arise indirectly from sin while some in addition may represent the direct results from sin. Sin produced humanity's fall. With the fall came human mortality, making our bodies subject to death processes which impair our function and eventually kill us. God had warned (" . . . when you eat of it you will surely die," Gen 2:17). But the warning was in vain. When tempted, first the woman, then the man fell into disobedience.

We can say then that all sickness arises indirectly from sin in the sense that sin has blighted our race as a whole, rendering us all subject to degeneration, to decay and to invasion by hostile organisms. What we must not always say is that Aunt Mary's rheumatism is a sign that Aunt Mary did something wicked or that God is punishing her with painful joints.

A direct relationship may or may not exist. Today I spent time with a man whose brain was so severely damaged by drinking and by neglect of a proper diet that he seems to have permanent difficulty in maintaining his balance, has problems with his vision and such a gross impairment of his memory that he cannot remember where he is sixty seconds after he has been told. His liver may eventually pack up entirely.

If perpetual drunkenness is sinful, then my patient's sickness arises from his sin. Likewise, if sexual promiscuity is sinful (and Scripture says it is), then the ravages of the sexually transmitted diseases which sometimes accompany promiscuity are the direct results of sin.

But there are less obvious ways in which personal sin can cause sickness. The apostle James seems to hint at them (Jas 5:15-16): "The prayer offered in faith will make the sick person well; the Lord will raise him up. If he has sinned, he will be forgiven. Therefore confess your sins to each other and pray for each other so that you may be healed."

And many Christians report instances where confession of sin has led to healing. Kurt Koch, for instance, writes of a farmer's dying wife who pleaded for an evangelical Christian to visit her that she might unburden herself before she died. During the visit for "a period lasting two hours, the woman made an open confession of her sins. She was now prepared to die. However events proved otherwise. Later when the Christian brother visited the farm again, he found the farmer's wife standing in the yard with a look of joy on her face. He could hardly believe his eyes. What had happened? It transpired that after she had confessed her sins, in addition to forgiving her, the Lord had also touched her body and healed her. Yet at the time of her confession the thought of healing had never entered her mind."

Thank you, Jesus, that you are ready to deliver me from spiritual bondage. Thank you that you also sometimes offer me physical healing. I want to live free from my sins and trusting you for true wholeness. Help me, I pray. Amen.

EIGHT. Demons and Mental Illness ◊

Our struggle is not against flesh and blood, but against the rulers, against the authorities, against the powers of this dark world and against the spiritual forces of evil in the heavenly realms.

EPHESIANS 6:12

Among modern Christians I find a wide range of attitudes about demons.

There are enthusiasts who seem overeager both to spot demons and to bind them, exorcise them or consign them to the outer darkness where they belong. Some enthusiasts claim a special "ministry" in the occult. At the other extreme are Christians who do not believe in demons at all.

Between the two extremes are those of us who are far less certain of ourselves. We believe demons exist. We believe they are still around. Yet in spite of our biblical and theological studies and our psychological sophistication, we are better at talking about demons than at spotting them or dealing with them. We are, as it were, neither fish nor fowl in the matter of demonology.

I have no question that demons are alive and well in the West today. But there are dangers in all three positions I outlined above.

We fight against principalities and powers. The foul hordes are about us. We ignore them at our peril. They will oppose the slightest attempt we make to follow Christ. Those who profess not to believe in them or who ridicule any concern about demons today will never prove effective soldiers of Christ. Evil is personal, potent, real and rampant.

But some enthusiasts are exposing themselves to danger, the danger of being mocked as fools by the very enemy they talk so much about, as well as the danger of doing more harm than good. They seek to cast out demons where sometimes no demons exist. They may unwittingly pander to the weak consciences of some who want an excuse (an obliging demon) for what amounts to personal sin that needs to be confessed and put aside.

Again, enthusiasts may pay more attention to Satan than to Christ and may be more occupied with his power than with the glory of Jesus. Or they may add greatly to the distress of Christians by calling on them to renounce and resist nonexistent demons. Some suffering souls are already the victims of debilitating sickness and now have foisted on them by their spiritual counselors an additional burden of guilt, false guilt about not resisting the dark powers enough.

Yet the middle-of-the-road position also has its dangers. We say we believe, but do we? To profess to believe that imminent peril exists but that we are unable either to see or to deal with the peril is a sorry position to be in. Are we perhaps respectable fence-straddlers? We cannot be accused of not taking Scripture seriously, for we say we believe. But our so-called belief would be impotent before the man possessed of many demons who tore the chains out of rock.

Perhaps we should be more willing to run the risk of being fools or of getting our hands dirty.

Lord Jesus, you calmed the man called Legion. Calm my many fears; cast out from me any demonic personages; help me to renounce Satan and all his henchmen and to listen well to the Holy Spirit. Amen.

NINE. The Panic Spiral ◊

Do not be anxious about anything.
PHILIPPIANS 4:6

As a recently graduated doctor I was given major duties in surgery too early. Within a year of completing my medical training I was frequently responsible at night for all the emergency surgery in a large city hospital as well as in a small hospital on one of Britain's major highways. During the day I was often given my own operating list. In less than a year after that I was doing gastrectomies.

Understandably, things sometimes went wrong—seriously wrong. In the operating room a wave of panic would occasionally begin to rise in me as with horror I would see that the operation was getting into a deeper and deeper mess. An unconscious patient's life depended on me. The anesthetist was competent in his or her own area but could offer me no help. Senior surgeons were an hour away. With the panic came a sort of freezing in my brain. My movements were hurried but pointless and repetitive. I would stare at the circle of the eyes of the assisting team, but all eyes would be looking silently back at me.

Under such circumstances the only thing I could do was forcefully to will myself to think slowly and deliberately. I discovered that being a Christian I had been sending up panicky prayers, "Oh Lord, help! Lord, don't let it go wrong! Lord, don't let me get into a mess! Don't let her die!" They were muttered incantations, not prayer. I had not been aiming at communicating with God but was simply expressing panic in parrot talk.

God of course was merciful. *He* was there. But I saw that I had to stop and think. On a spiritual level I had to talk to myself rather than to God. "God *is* here. He doesn't need to be badgered. He *does* care. Now take it easy. What's my *immediate* aim? What should I do first?"

Slowly, as I did this, a mental clearing came. My mind unfroze and I found myself, if not relaxed, at least able to be deliberate and calm. Slowly, with a sense of growing confidence and relief, I found my way through the difficulties, successfully completing what could have been a tragically botched operation. My mind had been freed to accept new ideas, to remember old principles and to force myself to rely on them and go ahead.

I have no doubt that God's Holy Spirit was behind it all. But what was demanded of me in each little crisis was to force myself to stop the panic spiral and think.

I keep forgetting you are with me all the time, Holy Spirit. Like now, for instance. Thank you. Let me carry the stillness of this moment into the rest of the day. When I forget and panic—please remind me again. Amen.

TEN. Human Beings: Great . . . But Lost ◊

So God created man in his own image, in the image of God he created him; male and female he created them.
GENESIS 1:27

What does it mean to be "made in the image of God"? To some it means that we possess certain attributes of God such as emotion, volition, intelligence and a sense of morality and ethics. Certainly the Scriptures portray us as having such qualities, including the ability to choose and a moral sense. According to the Scriptures we can make *some* real decisions (even though we may not be entirely free). In addition, we have had throughout our history a sense of "oughtness," a sense of right and wrong.

Others view the meaning of the phrase "in the image of God" differently. While acknowledging that the Bible as a whole attributes such qualities to humanity, they suggest that the phrase has more to do with our function on earth. Like God we are to rule. "Let them have dominion over the created order," God is heard to say in the beginning of the book of Genesis.

But from this lofty position of supremacy the man and woman sinned and fell. In that fall they were both morally and mortally wounded. Sin warped their personality. But it did more. It alienated them from God and distorted their relationship with creation. They now had to earn their food by painful toil. Sin also impaired (though did not destroy) their ability to think and to make decisions.

More serious still, sin, like a disease, not only made them mortal but made it impossible for them, in spite of their best resolutions, to refrain from sinning. And in this sense too we see them as a "down-from-above" man and woman.

We also see in them the shattered image of God. Shattered, but not totally gone. And—this is the great truth of the Christian gospel—by God's grace the image can be restored.

Father, receive my thanks for your love which created me in your own image. And, while sin has taken its heinous toll, I marvel at the restoration you offer through the cross of Christ. Be working that restoration in my life, I pray, by your great grace. Amen.

ELEVEN. The Hunger for the Holy ◊

Then Moses said [to the LORD], "Now show me your glory."
EXODUS 33:18

The best-known quote from St. Augustine is found in the first paragraph of the first chapter of the first book of his famous *Confessions:* "Thou hast made us for thyself and our hearts are restless till they find their rest in thee."

Where does this restlessness for God come from?

Over a period of time it became progressively more clear to me in my psychiatric practice that Man is "homo religiosus." While I was careful not to take advantage of my position as a physician, nor to impose my religious convictions on vulnerable patients, I knew that many of them had profound religious concerns which they longed to share with someone they could trust. The outlook of scientific humanism which has pervaded modern society has not diminished a longing for God. It has increased it.

People will always pay a price when that religious drive within them is stifled or frustrated. And in the wild potpourri of cults, new religions and the pop psychologies of the human potential movement, I see only evidence of people's hunger and thirst for a God they do not know. We human beings, whether we recognize it or not, have a yearning to know the holy God.

Lord, I yearn for a vital, true experience of you. Open me to your presence and glory. Amen.

TWELVE. Holy, Holy, Holy ◊

Who among the gods is like you, O LORD? Who is like you—majestic in holiness, awesome in glory, working wonders?

EXODUS 15:11

T he word *holiness* denotes God's differentness, his otherness. We often think of holiness as a sort of infinitely superior goodness. It is much more. Two elements are of special importance.

One is his inconceivableness. Theologians call it his *transcendence*. While God has made himself both real and close to those who believe in Christ (what theologians call *immanence*), we would never dare claim to understand God. A baby may know and enjoy the nearness of its mother, but it does not thereby comprehend her. And the gap preventing us from understanding God is far wider. Dizzy with its infinite span, Paul cries out, "How unsearchable his judgments, and his paths beyond tracing out!" (Rom 11:33).

The other aspect of God's holiness we would not have invented either—his moral perfection. By this we are not just implying that we give him top grades for keeping all the rules. We mean that he is free from all moral limitations. God is not holy because he obeys certain laws which define the difference between right and wrong. Those rules are himself! Before time was, he gave birth to the very quality that we call righteousness. Purity, faithfulness, mercy and lovingkindness are his inventions. The rules merely describe, dimly and imperfectly, what God is.

As you see, we could quickly tie ourselves into intellectual knots discussing God's holiness. We might get into a complex argument with an atheist friend. But one who catches the least glimmer of what holiness means can't be bothered with arguing about it any more than a man in love wants to argue about the existence of women. A very different experience engages all his attention. Holiness, you see, is easier *felt* than *telt*.

Perhaps that is why the Bible speaks most often about God's holiness in poetry, song and prayer—the languages of worship. It may be a reason, too, why we should approach the study of such passages not only with our minds alert but with our hearts bowed and still. For the infinite God is waiting to show some of his holiness to us.

Many tell me, Father, that right and wrong are outdated. But I know that right is right, because you are righteousness. Thank you for making this a moral universe. And thank you, O high and holy One, that you offer to walk with me through my life on earth. Amen.

THIRTEEN. Signposts ◊

You will be my witnesses.
ACTS 1:8

A signpost points to a destination. It matters little whether the signpost is pretty or ugly, old or new. It helps if the lettering is bold and clear. But the essential features are that it must point in the right direction and be clear about what it is pointing to.

If you ask people to describe the signposts that directed them to their destination, they will remember some and forget others altogether. But forgotten or remembered, the signposts will have done their job if they have got the traveler to where he wanted to go.

"Ye shall be witnesses unto me," Jesus told the early disciples. In a sense it matters very little whether you are an antiqued rural signpost written in elegant ancient script or a bright green modern one strung up high over the freeway. You do not exist to draw attention to yourself but to direct people's thoughts to a divine destination. A signpost has defeated its purpose if it is so attractive that it draws attention to itself rather than to a place.

Therefore remember that in witnessing, while you will be talking about your personal experience, giving as it were a firsthand report of your encounter with Christ, your witness will not focus on you but on the Christ you experience. Newly engaged persons may talk about their engagement in one of two ways. One will give a self-centered account of conquest, of parties—will be enamored more with the state of being engaged than with the person to whom he or she is engaged; another, while confessing his or her love, will speak in glowing terms of the person who has won them. Don't be enamored with the blessed state of being a Christian, but be enamored with Christ and confess what he means to you.

May His beauty rest upon me
As I seek the lost to win,
And may they forget the channel,
Seeing only Him. Amen.

FOURTEEN. Magnificent Insanity ◊

The kingdom of heaven is like a merchant looking for fine pearls. When he found one of great value, he went away and sold everything he had and bought it.

MATTHEW 13:45-46

There is a magnificent insanity about the parable in Matthew 13:45. It has to do with a pearl freak—a merchant whose hobby was pearls. Evidently, one day he came across a pearl to end all pearls. Imagine him with staring eyes, quickly taking in his breath, licking his dry lips, then anxiously inquiring about price, haggling and pondering the tremendous cost of the pearl.

You can also imagine him returning home and looking over the rest of his pearl collection. With shaking hands he would pick them up one by one and drop them into a soft leather pouch. Not only pearls, but house, slaves and everything would go so that the one pearl might become his.

And then, bereft of everything but a big pearl, what would the fool do? You can't eat pearls. In my mind is a picture of the crazy guy sitting in a miserable hovel—his glowing eyes feasting on his pearl and his fingers gently caressing it. Crazy? Perhaps he is the one sane person among us.

It all depends on whether the pearl was worth it. We see at once that treasure in heaven would be worth it. Why then are we so quick to opt for earthly treasure and so slow to be interested in the heavenly? Perhaps it is because we do not believe in heavenly realities. They represent a celestial cliché in our minds, but no more.

Only true faith will make us step along the way of the cross. And if we are to step lightheartedly, there will have to be the kind of faith which has become profound conviction that the joys are real and tangible, the next life is very important, and Jesus really is preparing a place on high.

The way of the cross is a magnificent obsession with a heavenly pearl, beside which everything else in life has no value. If it were a case of buying it, we would gladly sell all we had to do so.

But we cannot buy heavenly treasure. It is not for sale. The point of the parable is that having caught a glimpse of the pearl, we count all else of no value and pursue the treasure.

Lord, too many things win my heart. Please help me set other "treasures" aside and become obsessed with the treasure that never decays—divested of earth's riches and rich with heavenly realities. Amen.

FIFTEEN. A Partner with God ◊

Then the LORD said, "Shall I hide from Abraham what I am about to do? . . . All nations on earth will be blessed through him. . . . He will direct his children and his household after him to keep the way of the LORD."

GENESIS 18:17-19

What a partnership! God taking on a human being as his partner. Telling him the plans. Depending on his good performance. Using him—foibles and all—to bring about the great redemptive plan of heaven.

Now, God knew Abraham. He knew that Abraham would order his household in a godly fashion. He knew Abraham would instruct his children properly. Was God then selecting a superior human, one with whom he could have dealings, as distinct from the rest of us? The question is an important one. If we answer yes, then we must face a long struggle to upgrade our lives enough so God will feel it worth his while to share things with us.

God said, "For I know [Abraham]." The word *know* in Hebrew can be translated "choose" or "make . . . my friend." In saying he knows Abraham, God is saying, "I chose Abraham to be my friend. I have changed the relationship of Creator to creature, of Judge to sinner, and have added a new dimension to it. I have selected this man to be my friend. I also want him as a partner. He will have a role in my plans. Moreover, though I know he will keep my precepts and teach them to his children, I want him to be more than a yes man. I want him to be a true partner, sharing fully in those projects he will have a part in."

It may seem inconceivable that this same God wants such a relationship with you. You are a creature he made. You are a sinner he redeemed. You are even his child by adoption and by supernatural new birth. Yet he calls you to a higher dignity as well—that of friend and partner. "I no longer call you servants," Jesus told his disciples, "because a servant does not know his master's business. Instead, I have called you friends, for everything that I learned from my Father I have made known to you" (Jn 15:15). He *chose* you to be such.

Two facts necessarily follow. If you are his friend, he will share his thoughts and plans with you. If you are his partner, he will be concerned about your views on his plans and projects. Whatever else prayer may be, it is intended to be a sharing and a taking counsel with God on matters of importance to him. God has called you to attend a celestial board meeting to deliberate with him on matters of destiny.

You can see at once how this raises the whole level of prayer. It is not intended primarily to be centered in your petty needs and woes. To be sure, God is interested in them. They have a place on his agenda. But the agenda itself has been drawn up in heaven and deals with matters of greatest consequence.

Mighty God, you call me friend and partner! I find this astonishing. And I long to please you as I work together with you on kingdom concerns. Amen.

SIXTEEN. Security: True or False? ◊

Watch out! . . . a man's life does not consist in the abundance of his possessions.

LUKE 12:15

S ecurity. How we plan for it! We save. We invest. We are provident, responsible. We think of our old age and of our children's educations. Little by little we build our tiny fortresses, hiding from the threat of penury behind savings, locks and bolts. Recession? Some of us may be worried enough to invest in things we hope recession will not affect. Others among us smile secretly for we are experienced investors and feel we have solved the problem.

We are like the rich fool of Luke 12:15-21. Our professions and businesses have brought forth plentifully. We have more money than we need—even after giving our tithes. What can we do? We discuss matters carefully with our accountants, and having acted on sound advice we tell ourselves, "We now have ample reserves. Let us travel abroad in winter and spend our summers with the children. We have earned it. It's time we took things easy!"

The rich fool was not a fool for harvesting abundant crops. He was a fool for letting his crops fill his horizon and determine his lifestyle. He was a slave to barns and grain, and he seems to have had no interest in God.

When God's awful voice awakened him from his dreams saying, "You fool! This very night your life will be demanded from you. Then who will get what you have prepared for yourself?" he had to leave his barns and enter the Presence naked. Had he sent anything on in advance? Jesus didn't say. Presumably he had forwarded no treasure. His heart was back among his mountains of grain.

But notice what this story teaches. The thrust of Jesus' teaching does not deal with the virtues of poverty or the sin of riches. Rather he seeks to show us first *the greater value of heavenly treasure* and the folly of seeking earthly treasure. Then he warns us of the seductive power of riches, the love of which draws our hearts away from him and renders us incapable of serving him. Finally he upbraids us with the unbelief which underlies our anxiety about our material needs.

It becomes very clear where our only security is to be found.

Lord, there are times when I do not live as though my security is in you. Forgive me and allow me to see heaven more clearly. Amen.

SEVENTEEN. God the Spirit in the Material World ◊

The Spirit gives life; the flesh counts for nothing. The words I have spoken to you are spirit and they are life.

JOHN 6:63

The Bible describes God as *Spirit.* This is a strange expression for modern men and women. For us the word *nonmaterial* is almost the same as *nonexistent.* The only kind of reality we know is formed of mass and energy. The absence of these means nothingness. Nonexistence.

Yet the God of the Bible is declared to be the nonmaterial *source* of matter. He existed before there were human brains to think thoughts about him. In fact, he created human brains. In the same way as people invent computers and not merely the coded information stored electronically inside the computer, so God is much more than an idea in human brains. The whole human race could perish and its ideas be snuffed out like candles. But God would exist.

Instead of using words like *nonmaterial* (a negative term, yet one we understand), the Bible speaks of God as *Spirit* (a positive term we do not fully understand). We can't think of what "spirit" is any more than we can see the wind. Many of us form vague pictures in our minds of something that floats and fills space. Probably we will one day laugh at our concepts. Yet in the meantime it is comforting to know that we are not called to understand spirit but to *know* God the Spirit.

Two facts about the Spirit are key. The first is that the Spirit of God is more than an abstraction. He is a Person. He teaches (Jn 14:26). He can feel grief (Eph 4:30). He rebukes us and reveals things to us (Jn 16:8-11).

The second fact is that the Spirit is alive. Ideas, of course, are said to live when they cause changes in society. They are dead when they are forgotten. But God is not an idea, and he is alive in a much more important sense.

Biological life (the only kind we are acquainted with) is self-reproducing. Flowers give seed from which more flowers grow. Bacteria, viruses, humans and frogs all reproduce after their kind. It is apparent from Scripture that biological life provides us with an analogy for conceiving spiritual life. Even its capacity to reproduce itself is an echo of the more powerful and significant form of life, the spiritual. God the Spirit begets spiritual children (Jn 3:1-8). He begets them among human bipeds by planting the living seed of his Word in their hearts.

The vital energy of the life he imparts is so great that our character is changed. Men and women who have experienced spiritual rebirth are aware of a new force within them. Their friends become aware of it too—by change of behavior and even of faces. Such men and women are the sons and daughters of God in a quite literal sense. He has reproduced himself in them. Our minds reel to comprehend such thoughts, and our hearts leap that God loves us so.

Spirit of God, eternal living Person, praise be to you. You have given me life in my own spirit. You have shown me wonders far beyond the material world. You offer me unending life with you. Holy Spirit, receive my praise, in Jesus' name. Amen.

EIGHTEEN. Sweating for the Lord ◊

So we continued the work . . . from the first light of dawn till the stars came out. . . . Neither I nor my brothers nor my men nor the guards with me took off our clothes; each had his weapon, even when he went for water.

NEHEMIAH 4:21, 23

Nehemiah shared hardship with the workers. His beard would be clogged with grit, his eyes red with dust while sweat would leave streaks down his cheeks.

Spirituality is no substitute for sweat. Nehemiah's organizing ability, his coolness under stress and even his prayers would have been wasted had he not worked. Prayer may move mountains. But prayer and elbow grease are wonderful allies. They make projects hum.

Some people convey the impression that work is not spiritual, that spirituality and sweat are not partners but rivals. I appreciate their point. Activity, whether physical or mental, is no gauge for effectiveness. The Christian world is full of useless activity. There are rounds of pointless meetings that serve only to keep the saints from getting bored. But activity is not work. Work is activity in the Lord. And activity in the Lord may mean sweat.

Nothing has ever been done for God without work. Nor has anyone been greatly used unless he or she has worked to capacity. It is true that outstanding missionaries and evangelists have had spiritual power. But they worked as well. They made use of the fact that God was with them. High-octane gasoline is to make a car run, not to keep it in the garage.

Paul "worked harder than all of them" (1 Cor 15:10). Wesley often preached several times a day, traveling on horseback, on foot and in unsprung coaches. Jesus himself not only warned his disciples that "night is coming, when no one can work" (Jn 9:4) but once sank into such exhausted slumber on a boat that even a Galilean storm failed to rouse him. Buffeted by wind and lashed by rain and spray, his inert, soaking body lay slumped on a cushion in the stern. Only one who has worked to the point of exhaustion sleeps that deeply.

Some Christians are confused about the relation between prayer and work. I have heard it said, for instance, that Christian leaders should pray and study more, and work less. Perhaps so. But I do not like to hear it stated that way. Are prayer and study a form of mere relaxation? Christian leaders who do not sweat over their prayer and study, giving themselves to it as heartily as a beaver to building a dam, will not count for much.

Father, you know what my capacity for work is. Help me to understand it and to work wisely and without any selfish holding back. Show me how best to make my energies count in your kingdom work. Amen.

NINETEEN. Trained by Jesus ◊

We loved you so much that we were delighted to share with you not only the gospel of God but our lives as well, because you had become so dear to us.

1 THESSALONIANS 2:8

J esus *trained* his disciples or, if you like, he *disciplined* them. He did not entertain them with special musical numbers. He lived with them, ate with them, shared their sleeping and living quarters. He knew them intimately. They probably heard him preach the same sermons many times (sermons so packed with content that they needed repeated hearings).

He also gave them private tutorials. He sent them on mission assignments. He chose them, exposed his own life to them, leveled with them, warned them, prayed over them. He allowed himself to be crucified before their terrified gaze; he then rose and revealed himself to them. He reproved their fears and unbelief with the utmost gentleness—and then sent them out to conquer the world.

Likewise, when we train God's people, we cannot limit ourselves to weekly sermons, prayer meetings and occasional mission conferences or evangelistic outreaches. Training in godliness must be full-orbed. It includes love, example and vulnerability. Paul wrote to the Thessalonians that he and Silas and Timothy were ready to share with them not only the gospel message but also *their own selves.* Our whole life needs to be on view and available to those we wish to help follow Christ more closely.

Jesus, you allowed your whole life to be on public display, despite the fact that people misunderstood and sometimes mocked. Help me to dare to offer my life to others so they can grow in you. Help me to be honest and vulnerable for your sake. Amen.

TWENTY. Holy Laughter ◊

Shout with joy to God, all the earth! Sing the glory of his name; make his praise glorious!
PSALM 66:1-2

We were in the capital of Guangdong Province in mainland China. There we met a Pastor Lam, a sixty-year-old man who cares for a house church of eight hundred members. His house was on a narrow street that admitted only pedestrians and bicycles.

Even though the church was not government-approved and not supposed to exist, people in the street, seeing we were foreigners, asked us if we were looking for Lam's house and volunteered to show us where it was. Inside that shell of a house, smiling young people hurried to bring us tea.

Lam had been imprisoned twice for his faith. His second imprisonment had lasted twenty-five years, doing hard labor in the mines. I asked him how he felt about it, and joy poured out of him. "It was wonderful!" he cried. "I could have been killed many times, but God preserved my life. And I wasn't injured in the mine, even though men around me were maimed and killed. I even preached there!"

He spoke fairly good English and described something of his life to us. But the story, fascinating as it was, was hard to concentrate on, so amazed were we by the extraordinary joy that filled and overflowed from him. Three times the police had to interrogate him during the previous two weeks, but he had laughed with genuine merriment. "I will preach!" he cried. "They can only take me if the Lord lets them. And I will go on preaching about Jesus wherever I am!" It was not bravado. It was a quality of joy we had never encountered before.

My joy is in you, O Lord. My heart is light and my feet dance with your praises. All creation joins me in singing your glories. Amen.

TWENTY-ONE. The Worth of a Person ◊

Look at the birds of the air; they do not sow or reap or store away in barns, and yet your heavenly Father feeds them. Are you not much more valuable than they?

MATTHEW 6:26

I n the Judeo-Christian view our glory does not lie principally in our creativity or the architectural splendor of our civilizations. Instead everything springs from the "down-from-above" view of humanity. The noblest efforts of Christians and Jews have arisen from the idea that, however mean and humble, however unattractive and despised another human being might appear, we must remember we are dealing with someone created by God, in his very image.

Think of the names of the great London hospitals or those of many other great cities—St. Thomas's, St. Bartholomew's and a whole string of other saints—reminders that these hospitals are monuments to a high view of humanity. The poor and the suffering had to be sheltered and healed *because they were made in the image of God.*

Let me make myself clear. I am not attempting to vindicate Christians so much as to look at the effect of an idea—the idea that human beings derive their importance from their high origin and high destiny. And the influence of that idea has spread into society generally. Many of the social attitudes we claim as enlightened and moral came from this source. It remains a powerful reminder of a specific view of human life in the remarkable work of Mother Teresa in Calcutta.

Malcolm Muggeridge writes of visiting her, "I raised the point as to whether, in view of the commonly held view that there are too many people in India, it was really worthwhile trying to salvage a few abandoned children who might otherwise be expected to die of neglect. . . . It was a point, as I was to discover subsequently, so remote from her whole way of looking at life that she had difficulty in grasping it. The notion that there could be too many children was, to her, as inconceivable as suggesting that there are too many bluebells in the woods or stars in the sky. . . . To suppose otherwise is to countenance a death wish. Either life is always and in all circumstances sacred, or intrinsically of no account."

Lord, it is easy to think certain categories of people are less valuable than others. Perhaps the very old, or the very poor. Perhaps the very sick, or those not yet born. Yet you made them all and gave them your value. Implant that gigantic idea firmly in my soul and help me to reflect it with each person I meet today. Amen.

TWENTY-TWO. Prayers That God Rejects ◊

When you ask, you do not receive, because you ask with wrong motives.
JAMES 4:3

God, will you please kill my next-door neighbor? I hate him. I hereby place my faith in you that you will get him knocked down by a car tomorrow. I do not have the least doubt that you will bring this to pass. In Jesus' name. Amen!"

"God, please enable me to lie and deceive expertly so I can swindle the money I need out of my business partner. I ask it in absolute faith in the name of Jesus. Amen!"

You can see at once that God would not answer such prayers. The reason would not be due to their technical difficulty. "Accidents" cause him no problems. He can close a person's eyes to an approaching car as easily as to an approaching swindler. But such blasphemous requests do violence to the nature of God and his kingdom. He refuses to be the instrument of murderous hate or theft. He refuses in fact to be the instrument of anything or anyone.

You will tell me doubtless that you would not dream of making the kind of request I used in my examples. No matter. The examples may be extreme, but you can see the point. There are certain things God *will not* do, however great our faith may be.

When we pray, therefore, we must ask ourselves, "Am I requesting things that are consistent with God's nature, his designs, his kingdom, his will?" For prayer was not designed primarily for our comfort (though it can provide us with great comfort) but to enable us to collaborate with Christ in bringing about his kingdom.

Lord God, at times I offer prayers which do not please you. I repudiate now those longings which go against your will. I pray instead that you will by your great grace forgive me. And then, please use my prayers—and my life—toward the great goal of "Thy will be done." Amen.

TWENTY-THREE. Led Astray by Feelings? ◊

It is right for me to feel this way about all of you.
PHILIPPIANS 1:7

I n my youth as a Christian I was greatly helped by the story about Faith, Feelings and Facts, companions together along life's tricky pathway. The first two followed Facts who was in the lead. The story taught me that objective truth (Facts) was what mattered, and that my eyes of faith should be pinned on the facts, rather than on my emotions. Mr. Faith, you may remember, was often bothered when Mr. Feelings got into difficulties. However, when he took his eyes off Facts and turned to help Mr. Feelings, he himself invariably got into difficulties until he remembered that his job was to follow Facts, not to worry about Feelings. And according to the story, sooner or later Feelings would catch up.

The story teaches both a truth and a lie. The truth is that our faith is based on facts, not on feelings. The lie is that feelings always catch up.

For one thing, it is possible to be mistaken about the facts since Mr. Facts really represents one's own limited understanding of Scripture. It is always possible for our own grasp of facts to lead us astray, unless we are open to revise or refine it from time to time. And again, feelings are complex. Faith is only one of many factors influencing them. After all, if something so ordinary as a missed night's sleep or a bout of indigestion can affect them, what else might?

Yet research has made it clear that while careless giving way to emotional impulses can be harmful and destructive, many of us are sick, and some of us ultimately die because of repressed and overcontrolled emotions. They inflict horrendous damage on our cardiovascular and gastrointestinal symptoms. High blood pressure and ulcers of various kinds are closely linked with emotion. It is likely that there is not a bodily ailment which is not connected in some way with our hidden fears, our unexpressed griefs and our inability to rejoice without restraint.

The Lord means for us to pay attention to our feelings and express them appropriately, not to either exalt them or deny them.

Jesus, I ask you to be Lord of my emotions as well as of the other parts of my life. Thank you that you care about how I feel, not just how I act. Amen.

TWENTY-FOUR. Temptation But Not Dismay ◊

Each person is tempted when he is lured and enticed by his own desire. Then desire when it has conceived gives birth to sin.
JAMES 1:14-15 RSV

———————————————————————————————

There is no inconsistency between James' view that temptation is a man's inner lusts (inordinate internal desires) and the view that he is lured by Satanic appeal.

Have you ever fooled around with a piano? Open the top. Press the loud pedal. Then sing a note into the piano as loudly as you can. Stop and listen. You will hear at least one chord vibrating in response to the note you sang. You sing—and a string in the piano picks up your voice and plays it back.

Here, then, is a picture of temptation. Satan calls and you vibrate. The vibration is the "lust" James speaks of. Your desire is to go on responding to his call. If pianos have feeling, I imagine they are "turned on" when the cord vibrates. There is nothing bad about vibrating. The cord was made to vibrate and vibrate powerfully. But it was meant to vibrate in response to a hammer—not in response to a voice.

The appropriate response, then, is not to vibrate rapturously to the voice of the devil but to release the loud pedal and close the top of the piano. As Luther put it quaintly, you cannot stop birds from flying about your head, but you can prevent them from building a nest in your hair.

There are temptations which I simply need to walk away from, Lord. They aren't hard to figure out. They are plain; I know them. But they are hard to resist. By your grace, give me the strength to simply turn around and go another way. Amen.

TWENTY-FIVE. Choices ◊

You still lack one thing. Sell everything you have and give to the poor, and you will have treasure in heaven. Then come, follow me.

LUKE 18:22

Again and again in my life I have had to face choices. At one stage in my life it was English literature or Jesus. Though I was a medical student, I had a passion for literature. I even tried to collect first editions of Victorian novelists. I read late into the night, so late that I would be of no use the next day. Good literature was an escape for me. I was not reading it as it should be read but drugging my mind in soporific clouds of words.

But God had shown me something of his own treasures, and my heart craved them. In some dim way I perceived that my weakness for fiction interfered with my capacity to experience the joys of Christ. So I packed all the works of eighteenth- and nineteenth-century novelists and poets into a great crate and gave them to a friend who was majoring in English.

I was left with a sense of relief and gratitude. I have never questioned the sanity of that decision. Today, books are crammed untidily on all my bookshelves and litter every room in my house. They no longer hinder me as they once did.

I suppose the choice I made was a sacrifice. Yet I saw it as a matter of what I longed for more.

Thank you, Father, for the incredible riches you offer. Help me to know what "selling all" means for me, right now, and to do it, for I do crave your treasures. Amen.

TWENTY-SIX. Praying Through ◊

The priests and the Levites stood to bless the people, and God heard them, for their prayer reached heaven, his holy dwelling place.
2 CHRONICLES 30:27

I f you approach God with the determination to *pray through* a request, as though success in prayer depends upon your determined efforts, you are likely to wind up deeply discouraged.

A good deal depends of course on how one interprets the expression *pray through.* To some people it means to wait for God so that one might find clarity in the midst of confusion, an understanding of God's outlook, a changed perspective. Such praying through can only be good.

But to other people *praying through* means forcing your way against resistance until you get through to God. It means battering your bleeding knuckles against the portals of heaven until you gain access. If this kind of praying through were merely an exercise in futility or masochism, it would not be so bad. In actuality it not only discourages the person who prays, sometimes driving him to despair; it also dishonors God.

Someone might say to me, "Yes, but is it not true that the powers of darkness resist our prayers and that we may need to overcome Satanic opposition?"

I can recall only one instance in Scripture where demonic opposition impeded an answer to prayer. You can read about it in Daniel 10. I think it is naive to compare ourselves with Daniel, that great prayer warrior. In any case, Daniel was not battering his way through to God's presence. He was not involved with any kind of battle. He was simply so overwhelmed with sorrow that for three weeks he mourned and fasted. The battle that was going on was being fought in heavenly places. Daniel was not fighting it.

Nor is it possible to work up the state of mind which overwhelmed Daniel. He mourned and fasted because he could not help doing so. His state of mind was God-produced. Therefore if you must engage in prayerful shadowboxing, don't quote Daniel as your excuse.

It is always wrong to work up some kind of state of pseudofervor. It is carnal. It is self-defeating. It will get you nowhere. Its end result will be either spiritual pride or profound discouragement. From this arises another principle. Where you do not experience profound emotion in prayer, ignore your emotions. Faith is *an attitude of will* which says, "Whether I feel that God is there or not, whether I feel he will heed me or not, his Word tells me he hears and answers and I am going to count on that."

Lord, I want to wait for you, not to force my way into your presence. You know the desperate needs I want to tell you about. Help me to trust not in my ability to pray, but in your sovereignty and love. Amen.

TWENTY-SEVEN. Is It Okay to Be Rich? ◊

Jesus answered, "If you want to be perfect, go, sell your possessions and give to the poor, and you will have treasure in heaven. Then come, follow me."

MATTHEW 19:21

We often measure spirituality by doing without. Like any false notion, the idea is a half-truth. Jesus left riches in glory and embraced poverty that we might be made rich. He calls us to forsake all we have to follow him.

Notice two things. First, he calls *all of us* to forsake all and follow him. Just as there is no division between those who do sacred and those who do secular work, so none exists between those who are supposed to give up everything to follow him and those who are merely to give tithes and offerings. There is one standard of sacrifice applying equally to every child of God. No one is exempted from it. Any of us who claims to be exempt denies the righteous claims of Christ on his or her life.

Second, to give up everything for Christ consists of an *internal relinquishment* of all our possessions. The standard set before us is not that all Christians take a vow of poverty. Some of us will always be richer and others poorer. Yet all of us are to have a contract with Christ that whenever obedience to him means sacrifice of any degree, even to losing everything we have or to facing prison and death, then obedience is what matters. The obedience will be all the easier if we daily relinquish to him all we possess.

Lord, all I have is yours, not just a tenth. Show me how to use your possessions for your kingdom and glory. Amen.

TWENTY-EIGHT. God Our Father ◊

You received the Spirit of sonship. And by him we cry, "Abba, Father." The Spirit himself testifies with our spirit that we are God's children.
ROMANS 8:15-16

Superb teacher that he is, the Spirit knows we grasp most readily ideas based on our own experience. He teaches us, for example, that God is both Father and fatherly. Once again we must beware of the pseudointellectual trap of saying that God isn't *really* a father, but that this concept helps make him more real to us if we learn to think of him in that way.

On the contrary, God is the original Father—the fountain of fatherhood (Eph 3:14-15)! All the fine and meaningful things about human fathers are but feeble copies. A human father may melt inwardly as he watches his young children at play. But this is nothing compared to God's overflowing tenderness as he looks down on his children. And the pain a human father may feel when his child rejects his love and walks away is nothing to the anguish God knows when we forsake him.

The concept of God as Father leaps to life in the book of Hosea. Few things fill a human father so full of emotion as helping his first baby to walk. "It was I who taught Ephraim to walk," God says, lamenting that the child has now forsaken him (Hos 11:3). So deep and fierce are God's fatherly yearnings that he longs to acquire more sons and daughters and to bring back to him those who have wandered away. Like the father of the prodigal son, he waits on the road, searching the horizon for the return of the one who was lost, ready to run and throw out his arms in welcome. If there is but the glimmer of desire and willingness on our part to come to him in humility and repentance, then the God who is holy beyond our comprehension, the God who is Spirit yet the highest reality, the God whose wrath and compassion far surpass ours—this loving Father will not delay in revealing himself to us.

Thank you, heavenly Father, that you are not a metaphor but a very real father to me. Please enable me to accept your love, your discipline, your comfort when I sorrow, your ready forgiveness when I return from wandering. Amen.

TWENTY-NINE. Overworked or Overstressed? ◊

In vain you rise early and stay up late, toiling for food to eat—for he grants sleep to those he loves.
PSALM 127:2

While you can work too much, it is not true that you can emphasize work too much. Work does not produce nervous breakdowns, despite what anyone may have told you to the contrary. Work as hard as you like and as long as you like. If you're in normal health, you come to little harm, especially if your labor is in the Lord.

Why? Because it is tension that kills, not work. It is getting caught in the Christian rat race that does the damage. It is the desperate fight to keep up a front with Christian friends or with the Christian public, to appear smilingly spiritual and "produce" spiritually when you know all the while that your true inner life does not measure up to your exterior image.

Sometimes we work too much not because the work is essential, but because we are driven by *fear* rather than sustained by *faith*. Workaholics are driven. Work for them is not an expression of faith but a search for peace. Whereas some people seek to be justified by works, workaholics try to keep their consciences clean by working. Consequently they work too much and become slaves to their own neuroticism. Workaholics cannot easily rest; they begin to look haunted when relaxing and turn every leisurely activity into a new type of achievement that must be worked at and mastered.

The Scriptures do not encourage this sort of drivenness.

May I work for you, Lord, and not because of a neurotic need to achieve. Grant me energy to do your will. Amen.

THIRTY. For Love's Sake ◊

Mary . . . sat at the Lord's feet listening to what he said.
LUKE 10:39

What reasons can I give for the value of meeting regularly with God? Certainly we will escape the pettiness of the earthbound and commune with ultimate wisdom, infinity and love. Yet not even for these reasons, but for love's sake, would I urge us to meet God daily!

> As the deer pants for streams of water,
> so my soul pants for you, O God.
> My soul thirsts for God, for the living God.
> When can I go and meet with God? (Ps 42:1-2)

For love's sake we must seek him. For what he is, not for any advantage we may gain. Our quest must be the quest of a suitor, a suitor too blinded by beauty to descend to calculating self-interest, too intoxicated with love to care about the cost or the consequences of his suit.

It must be the love of Mary, sitting at Jesus' feet, enchanted by his words and grace, but deaf and blind to the frustration and fuss of her resentful sister (Lk 10:38-42). An enchantment of that sort will not be broken, nor its pleasures denied.

> One thing I ask of the LORD,
> this is what I seek:
> that I may dwell in the house of the LORD
> all the days of my life,
> to gaze upon the beauty of the LORD
> and to seek him in his temple. (Ps 27:4)

It is time we threw spiritual pragmatism out of the window. We come habitually to God carrying shopping baskets and armed with a checklist of needed purchases when all the time he wants to put his arms round us and draw us to himself. We know no other way. Custom and tradition have drilled us in the art of celestial bargain hunting.

It is time we forgot about our spiritual performance and our spiritual needs and gave ourselves up to passion.

Living God, I do love you. I do want your arms round me, more than I want my shopping list of prayer requests answered. Please draw me close and help me learn to dwell with you. Amen.

MONTH
TWO

ONE. The Way of the Cross ◊

Jesus . . . for the joy set before him endured the cross, scorning its shame.
HEBREWS 12:2

J esus' goal was to know the will of the Father and to do it. It was his aim both because he loved the Father and because he loved us. In consequence, Christ lived a life shadowed by the awareness that an early death awaited him. In doing the Father's will, he would be cut down as a man in his prime. To redeem the world he loved, he knew he faced a criminal's death, a violent and shameful death. Late in his public ministry, he even knew precisely when this would take place.

Yet, paradoxically, his outlook on life was positive and joyous, not in spite of the awful shadow so much as *because* of it. The shame of the cross was something he despised, knowing that it would not only prove a supreme triumph but also win him the object of his love. The writer to the Hebrews makes this clear.

I do not mean that Jesus experienced neither horror nor agony. He experienced both. But he chose the cross because it was the price he had to pay for something that was supremely important to him. The price might be incredibly high, higher than for anything else ever bought, yet Christ determined to get what he wanted. What was it he wanted? He wanted to please the Father and he wanted us. Think of it. Father, Son and Holy Spirit want fellowship with us. For Christ the cost was worth the bargain. You may not feel that fellowship with you is worth much, but Christ values your fellowship very highly indeed.

We make a great mistake then when we pity Christ on the cross. Astonishment—Yes! Wonder and amazement—Yes! Adoration and awe—Yes! Even tears. But pity—Never!

Christ Jesus, I am astonished by the awful price you paid. But it was a cost you embraced willingly. For it would purchase our salvation, our union, our communion, our fellowship, our oneness with you. Praise God. Amen.

TWO. Science and the Saints ◊

What may be known about God is plain. . . . For since the creation of the world God's invisible qualities—his eternal power and divine nature—have been clearly seen, being understood from what has been made.

ROMANS 1:19-20

There is a love-hate relationship between Christians and science. We fear science yet we worship it. If science "discovers" something that threatens Scripture or, which is much more likely, that threatens our favorite interpretation of Scripture, then science becomes the Enemy. Parents protest the way it is taught in schools. We busily create Christian schools and Christian universities for which, embarrassingly, we need to import Christian professors trained in godless universities.

On the other hand, if science discovers something that supports our favorite interpretations of Scripture, we discard our hostility and hail science as the latest and most reliable champion of the faith. After all, if science proves the Bible, the Bible must be true.

Most of us understand little about science, have too great a respect for it and overestimate its power both to undermine and to build up our faith. Science has little power to do either. It is true that some teachers of science use "scientific" arguments against faith, just as some Christians use "scientific" arguments to "prove" faith. But teachers of science and Christian apologists are human beings, and it is their human insecurity which sometimes is at work, not their scientific aptitudes.

Science is simply a useful way of looking at certain problems. It is limited in scope. It cannot bring about world peace, remove death or "discover" God. And while its application may add to the available supply of goods and services, it can do little to see that they are equitably distributed.

Christians need have no fear of science provided we remember three things. First, scientists are merely investigating the laws of our Creator. They sometimes make serious mistakes in their investigations and arrive at wrong conclusions. But if they pursue matters far enough, they can only find truth, for truth is all there is to find. But because scientists make mistakes, all scientific conclusions must be tentative. Sooner or later the most unshakable and the most firmly founded ideas crumble and fall.

Consequently, it matters little whether science supports Scripture or not. If today's science opposes, we need not fear for today's theory will be replaced by another tomorrow. By the same token it is unwise to rejoice in science's support of Scripture. Who are scientists that they presume to "confirm" the Word of the living God?

Finally, science is only one of many ways of discovering truth and has serious limitations. It becomes dangerous only when we worship it, that is, when we assume it is the high road to all understanding. When it comes to life's deepest questions (why do I exist? why is there a universe? does life have any meaning? how can I determine what is important in life?), science can offer us no help.

Creator God, thank you for what I see of you in the world and its natural laws. Thank you for revealing yourself beyond those as well, in your Word. You are far beyond my small understanding, O Lord. In spite of that, and because of that, I worship you. Amen.

THREE. The Personalness of Guidance ◊

I will instruct you and teach you in the way you should go; I will counsel you and watch over you.
PSALM 32:8

God's guidance is not mechanical.

Some people predict a time when all automobile traffic will be guided by computers. You will be able to get into your car, press a button, and somebody or something somewhere will guide you to work. You won't have to do anything. Your car will not get too near to the car ahead, and the car behind will not get too near to you. You won't even have to worry about whether you're going along the right street because the computer will direct you along an alternate route if traffic is too heavy on the one that you would normally use.

I don't know whether that will ever happen, though some planners and dreamers say it will. But such guidance isn't personal, and there is no comfort to be drawn from it. Oh, I suppose you can feel sort of safe, but it's not the feeling you get when your neighbor says, "Come, I'll show you where the store is." If you are a new student on campus, bewildered by the new environment and strange procedures, what a relief to hear someone say, "I'll show you where the university bookstore is, and then I'll show you where you register"! The personal contact brings enormous comfort.

The heart and core of the guidance God gives is bound up in the personal relationship he wants to have with us. We don't have to look in the morning newspaper for the horoscope and try to figure out who the dark stranger is. Apart from being superstitious, that is impersonal. God's guidance is "him and me." He wants to guide me. He is interested in me. Not a sparrow falls to the ground without his knowing it. He knows all about me and all about my problems, all about my sins and all about the mess I've made. And he still wants to guide me. Herein lies the preciousness of guidance.

In Psalm 32:9 we read, "Be not like a horse or a mule, without understanding, which must be curbed with bit and bridle." Today the psalmist might say, "Be not like an automated car controlled by a computer that can't think for itself, that must be directed by a program." Instead the Lord says, "I will counsel you with my eye upon you" (Ps 32:8 RSV). He watches and instructs and guides us individually.

Receive my gratitude, Lord, for this amazing truth: that you love me on a one-to-one, first-name basis and that you are willing to guide me in the same way. Be with me today and direct me in the decisions I face, for your glory. Amen.

FOUR. Demonic Power and Divine Power ◊

Each one threw down his staff and it became a snake. But Aaron's staff swallowed up their staffs.
EXODUS 7:12

We see power, *spiritual* power, in the classical struggles between the prophets and the sorcerers, between Moses and the magicians of Egypt, Daniel and the astrologers of Babylon, Joseph and the wise men of Pharaoh's court. And Yahweh's power always wins.

The Scriptures recognize a primal and a subsidiary source of power. First, there is Yahweh, the Creator of all, from whom all things and beings come and by whom they all consist. Then there are fallen angelic beings, banned from his presence by reason of their wicked rebellion. Milton paints vivid word pictures of their fall. They are the "principalities and powers" of the air, purveyors of temptation, tragedy and deception, still wielding and even offering to men and women the powers they embezzled from heaven.

Because the ultimate source of power is and can be only one, manifestations of power, whether from its principal and original source or from the rebels who absconded from heaven with large quantities of it, will have the same basic characteristics. *Demonic power is nothing more than divine power corrupted.*

Water that is dangerously polluted does not cease to be water and may still look like, feel like and even sometimes taste like pure water. So devilish miracles, visions, dreams and so on may be very similar in type, but terribly different in their ultimate effects on human beings. The similarity will deceive "even the very elect." Satan will appear "as an angel of light." Hell's power will, however, be progressively enslaving and end in death and destruction, while God's power will be redemptive, vivifying, cleansing, freeing and restorative.

Lord God Yahweh, I tremble at the greatness of demonic power. And I pray against it in the name of Jesus, rejoicing that your righteous, redemptive power always wins over the evil one's. Amen.

FIVE. Facing the Tempter ◊

Resist the devil, and he will flee from you.
JAMES 4:7

S atan tempts *from behind*. "Look," he whispers, "Isn't it beautiful? Just think what you could do . . . what people would say . . . how you would be admired . . . how much power you would have . . . look, *look*, LOOK!" The Bible gives us two complementary counsels, one on temptation itself and the other on the tempter. Concerning temptation we are simply told: Flee temptation. Concerning the tempter the word is: Resist the devil, *and he will flee from you.*

Think how these two counsels work together. Did you ever run away from something and face it at the same time? How could you?

Never face temptation. Flee from it. And in fleeing, *turn* your back on it. And in turning, whom will you face? Who has been standing behind you and whispering vivid word pictures in your ear? Turn and face him. Resist him. And his Satanic Majesty will withdraw.

But how do you resist?

Well, turning is three-quarters of the battle. Then unsheath your sword—"the sword of the Spirit . . . the Word of God."

When Jesus was tempted in the wilderness he responded to each Satanic suggestion with the words, "it is written . . . it is written . . . it is written." Each time that Jesus employed the sword of the Spirit, he slashed the tempter. Many Christians have testified to the astonishing effect particular Scriptures have in their ability to cope with temptation. The Bible is called the sword of the Spirit for three reasons: The Spirit inspired it; the Spirit will place it in your hands and teach you skill in using it; the Spirit will make it cut deep. Therefore get to know Scripture. And as you turn your back on temptation and face your tempter, reach out your hand for the sword which the Spirit will place in your grasp. Then plunge it deep into the tempter and hear him howl in pain as he flees back to hell.

Help me to hide your word in my heart, Lord, that I might not sin against you. Amen.

SIX. When Not to Praise God ◊

Woe to those who call evil good and good evil.
ISAIAH 5:20

Have you never praised God that Sasha tried to commit suicide? Have you never praised him that she drinks so much?"

Jean was shocked. But, desperate, she was ready to clutch at straws. She knew enough of the Bible to be dubious about the theology of the suggestion, but she could not resist the force of her friend's enthusiasm and her glowing accounts of "deliverance through praise power."

"God *has* to respond to praise! He can't resist it! What's more, the devil can't stand it. Demons take flight. Just praise him, Jean! Praise him for the mess she's in. Praise him because you're torn in two and can't stand it any more! Praise him that he will come in and take over!"

The example I quote is not extreme. People have said similar things to me personally. On a number of counts I damn their advice as God-dishonoring and harmful. It may lift my mood but only by a psychological trick.

First, we are not called on to praise God for evil. *He* does not rejoice in it and neither should we. To praise him for it is like praising a mother because her baby has been run over by a car. It is as revolting as it is inappropriate.

Second, praise is an expression of trust and gratitude, not a technique for exerting pressure on God. Not all Christians put it as explicitly as Jean's friend, but there are books that do. I know that in some places the Bible depicts God as "repenting of his evil" in response to human repentance and earnest prayer. But nowhere is praise seen as a weapon placed in the hands of human beings to make God do something human beings want him to. You can't manipulate God with any technique. Praise power, as it is currently taught and practiced, is a form of blasphemy. It reduces God to a celestial vending machine. Insert some praise, select the right button, then get whatever you want.

God cannot be manipulated. But he can occasionally be provoked by such attempts. Once his people "gave in to their craving; in the wasteland they put God to the test. So he gave them what they asked for, but sent a wasting disease upon them" (Ps 106:14-15). A wise parent may occasionally do the same thing, letting a child learn from bitter experience how detestable is the very thing that had looked so desirable. We may know what we want. We may even succeed (if we are foolish enough) in getting what we want. But before we praise God, let us be sure that we are in tune with him and that anything we request coincides with what he wants for us and for our children.

May I praise you, God, for who you are and the things you desire. Forgive me for trying to get out of you what I want. Teach me instead to listen to your will for me. Amen.

SEVEN. Believing Is Seeing ◊

Shout for joy to the LORD, all the earth, burst into jubilant song with music.

PSALM 98:4

What better place could there be for the release of our pent-up emotions than before the throne of grace? Yet some Christian leaders can scream with delight or howl with rage at football games but never think of shouting "to God with cries of joy" (Ps 47:1). Our Christian culture has too often made it difficult for us to shout for joy, even when it would be appropriate to do so. In fact I ask myself: Are most conservative Christians scared of emotion? If so, why? We should be scared of emotionalism, the artificial manipulation of emotion. But emotion itself? Let me lay down the basic principle.

Emotion comes from seeing, from understanding. I experience fear when I realize I might die during the operation the surgeon has suggested to me. The depth of my fear measures the clarity with which I see. My fears will be healthy if what I "see" truly corresponds with reality, for emotion is a test of my grasp of reality. Emotions do not save me—except in the sense that they may startle and shake me into acting in the light of truth.

When the Holy Spirit awakens people, he seems to cause them to perceive truth more vividly. Satan's deceptive mists are driven away. People see their sin as terrifying rocks threatening to sink them or as a foul, stinking cancer that will kill them. They see the mercy of the Savior with the eyes of those who have been snatched from a horrible death. Their trembling, weeping and shouts of joy reflect the clarity of their vision.

You can be so afraid of your feelings that you impair your capacity for truth. Scripture rings with the cries of people's hearts, their longings, their fears, their exultations and adorations. We begin to die the moment we refuse to feel. What we must fear is any carnal or evil source of our feelings, or any tendency to place our faith in our feelings rather than in God's Word.

The antithesis in Scripture is not between feelings and faith, but between sight (having to do with visible external reality) and faith. We say "seeing is believing," whereas Scripture teaches us "we live by faith, not by sight" (2 Cor 5:7).

Open my eyes, Lord, that I may see my sin as you see it and your love as you know it. Then move my heart in repentance and worship. Amen.

EIGHT. The Sum of My Years ◊

For whoever wants to save his life will lose it, but whoever loses his life for me will save it.
LUKE 9:24

O ne night when I was sixteen, I was too excited to sleep. For the first time I saw the years of my life as a lump sum. Whereas many people spend their lives a few weeks at a time, squandering life aimlessly on whatever would catch their attention, I wanted to use the total sum of my years to purchase something big. Exciting fantasies swept over the screen of my imagination. Then, in a moment of wonder and gratitude, it occurred to me that I could hand my years in their entirety to Christ to be disposed of in whatever way he chose. I knelt by my bed and did so.

My decision was not a noble one. In part at least it was based on self-interest. Yet Christ mercifully took me at my word and repeatedly brought me back to that same decision.

I did not realize at the time that there was nothing mechanical about the contract between us. I supposed that having handed my years to him I would have no further say in the matter, and that automatically he would take the years from me, since they were his.

And so they were. My years truly belonged to him, and I had wholeheartedly acknowledged the fact. But I found I was still the administrator of them. Since they came to me one at a time, indeed one day at a time, I could only pay my debt in small installments. Jesus understood this when he said that belonging to him means denying ourselves and taking up our cross *daily*. And this meant that the impulsive choice of a moment on a hot August night had to become the choice of every moment that followed.

Happily, Christ wanted to set me free even more than I wanted to be set free. And though, like everyone around me, I failed all too often to pay him what I owed, he pursued me relentlessly, teaching me in the thousands of small choices that I made how freedom could be found.

Lord, I do want my years and my days to belong to you. Help me to offer them up one day at a time and to administer them wisely, choice by choice by choice. Amen.

NINE. Belonging ◊

Many will say to me on that day, "Lord, Lord, did we not prophesy in your name, and in your name drive out demons and perform many miracles?"

MATTHEW 7:22

To whom do we belong? We belong in practice to whomever or whatever receives our allegiance.

We owe our allegiance to Christ. None of us would deny it. But the essence of unfaithfulness lies in looking to other sources for what our true bridegroom gives us freely.

Do we or do we not belong to him? The question is a solemn one, for in my ears I hear querulous voices of the future pleading, "Lord, did we not organize rallies in your name and in your name bring thousands to the Exhibition Hall? Lord, did we not put on a television show that brought in thousands of dollars for your cause?" And for some of these the answer will be, "Depart from me, you workers of iniquity, into outer darkness. For I never knew you."

The truth is, we do belong to Christ. Therefore, what will he not give? Does he not now sit at the right hand of God? Has he not told us that all authority in heaven and earth lies between his fingers? Is he not the author whose writing creates the history enacted before our eyes?

Has he not sent his Spirit? Is the Spirit not even this moment working in the minds and hearts of millions who as yet have heard no word of Christian testimony? Did he or did he not rise from the tomb? Did he or did he not make the sun stand still, open the waters of the Red Sea, cause the walls of Jericho to fall with a trumpet blast? Has he not for twenty centuries created revivals, reformations and awakenings without any mechanical aid that we could devise?

We are the followers of the Triune God of the Universe. We tread in the footsteps of apostles and martyrs. We do not gauge the success of our preaching by the number of our converts but by its clear adherence to the truth. We are those who are to be filled with the Holy Spirit. We would rather be laughed to scorn and thrown to the lions than descend to gimmicks and trickery to turn on a crowd at an evangelistic meeting. We are clothed in garments of salvation. Angels and demons look on to see what we will do. We bear the mark of God upon our foreheads. We are citizens of heaven, future judges of the universe, fellow heirs with Christ. Let us beware lest we forget the high dignity of our calling.

You are a great God, O Lord. May my life give you praise, honor and blessing. Amen.

TEN. An Angry God ◊

The LORD will cause men to hear his majestic voice and will make them see his arm coming down with raging anger and consuming fire . . . the breath of the LORD, like a stream of burning sulfur, sets it ablaze.

ISAIAH 30:30, 33

One man speaks of "the kind of God I would feel comfortable with." Perhaps all of us try to, or would like to, make God in our own image. We may not carve him out of wood, but we do try to forget the unpleasant parts of him and shape him to our personal comfort. We make him into a sort of holy teddy bear.

We may be bothered by the idea of an *angry* God because we know what our own anger is like. The matter may be complicated because we were taught that anger is innately evil. Certainly our human anger can be a vicious, evil, ugly thing. It's inconceivable to think of God as having that same guilt-provoking rage.

But there we go again creating God in our own image. We read into

God's anger what we experience of our own. Yet God's anger is altogether unlike ours. His anger is against evil. All evil. Everywhere. Always. My anger is often about trivia.

I get mad when I'm frustrated. My pencil snaps for the fourth time in a row, or the man in front of me stalls at a stoplight while the cars behind me honk impatiently. God's pencils do not break. Honking cars do not perturb him. He is never frustrated, never in a hurry.

At other times I get angry because I'm uncertain about my position or feel insecure. When people disagree with my argument I begin to shout, because I have a deep, nasty fear that they may be right after all. God is not insecure. He never gets upset.

Or I may get angry because I can't control people. Wives get angry when they can't control their husbands' embarrassing behavior in public. Husbands rage because they can't always stop their wives from "running the show."

Only God has the right to control people. And often he chooses not to because he has made men and women in his own image and given them the responsibility of choice. But God is almighty. The problem of control, selfish or otherwise, doesn't exist for God.

There are times when we have every right to be angry. But when in our anger we behave with cruelty and a vicious lack of control, we are appalled by the sometimes irreparable damage we have done. We stare in dismay at the wreck of a lifelong friendship or weep over the final alienation of a child or parent. It was not that the anger was wrong, but that we could not control it and recklessly let it energize destructive sin.

God never loses his temper. Where the Bible talks about God's anger "waxing hot," it is using a literary device. God does not have a physical ear to hear, nor a physical arm to make bare. And his anger neither waxes nor wanes. "Waxing hot" makes it simpler for us to understand. But his anger, like everything else about God, is immutable, timeless, eternal.

Therefore we must not fall into the trap of supposing that the ugly things that torment us also torment God. God's anger is different from ours. Yet God is still an angry God. And anger is *sometimes* a good thing.

God, it frightens me to see your fierce anger. I cringe at following the God of

White-Hot Rage. Thank you that your anger is right, it is not out of control, and it deals powerfully with evil. Help me learn to handle my own anger in ways that honor you. Amen.

ELEVEN. War and Peace ◊

We implore you on Christ's behalf: Be reconciled to God.
2 CORINTHIANS 5:20

I s reconciliation at the heart of the gospel? "Any theology which is faithful to the church of Jesus Christ . . . cannot but be a theology of reconciliation, for reconciliation belongs to the essential nature and mission of the Church in the world," writes Tom Torrance. Reconciliation means replacing a state of war with one of peace. Whereas hostility and alienation separate, reconciliation restores harmony and closeness.

We are at war. We are each at war within ourselves. We are also at war with one another, and ultimately, we are at war with God. The breakdown began at the dawn of our history when we sinned and fell.

Reconciliation is that process by which hostility is abolished and peace restored. It is God replacing war with peace, alienation with friendship and intimacy.

But let us re-emphasize that the alienation is multidirectional. When Adam lost his peace with God, he lost his peace with himself. When Eve sinned she lost both her internal peace and her closeness to her husband. As we shall see later, this holds true throughout biblical history. Peace with God, peace with ourselves and peace with our neighbors (even peace with our physical environment) are inseparably linked. To lose one is to lose all. To regain *the* one (peace with God) is to begin to regain all.

Lord, I want peace on all fronts. Yet I sometimes enter battle when I do not need to. *Forgive me for ignoring the reconciliation you have provided; help me become not a warmonger but a peacemaker. And may others, seeing that, come to you for peace. Amen.*

TWELVE. The Place of Intellect and Art ◊

Love the Lord your God with all your heart and with all your soul and with all your mind.
MATTHEW 22:37

T he way of the cross is not a denial of the value of intellectual activity. Some Christians say to me, "We don't believe in higher education. It is worldly." But it is not higher education that is worldly, only ambitions of better jobs and prestige or intellectual and academic snobbery. It is true that knowledge puffs up, and it is true that many Christians lose out because of their academic ambitions. These dangers arise, however, not when we pursue but when we prostitute learning. Nothing in Scripture cancels the advice for us to "get knowledge, get understanding." In Christ's army, scholars and carpenters march shoulder to shoulder. No calling gets a higher rating than any other. It is our *motive* in pursuing the calling, whether academic or manual, that matters.

And the way of the cross is not a denial of the value of artistic expression.

Insofar as human nature is corrupt, creativity can be put to corrupt uses. Had you been a Hebrew in Joshua's day, you would have had to destroy pictures and statues captured in battle. You would have destroyed them because you were vulnerable to raw idolatry and demonism, living in an age in which the belief in evil deities and in their dwelling in images was strong. Modern archaeologists and art historians might weep over the "priceless" treasures lost to posterity, but your responsibility at that point in history was to preserve something of greater value for posterity—the knowledge of the one true God, who did not dwell in images made by humans. The loss of archaeological artifacts was a small price to pay to keep that of far greater worth.

Whether every puritanical assault upon the visual arts was justified, I cannot say. I raise the point because many devoted Christians for one reason or another have regarded all artistic expression as suspect except the composition of "Christian" music, hymn writing and the writing of Christian novels and such. Without realizing it, many Christians measure spirituality in terms of cultural and artistic impoverishment, which is hardly what God intended.

The One whose creative genius gave us the awesome spectacle of stellar galaxies and the fragile beauty of snow crystals and orchids made us to be, like him, creators too. The danger of art is that we begin to worship artistic expression itself, instead of receiving it thankfully from his hands or giving it to him in worship. And for that danger we must always watch.

Creator God, may I use all my creative energies to serve and glorify you. Focus my efforts this day on giving you praise in my life. Amen.

THIRTEEN. The Place of Pleasure ◊

Endure hardship with us like a good soldier of Christ Jesus.
2 TIMOTHY 2:3

T he way of the cross is not a denial of the rightness of pleasure. God invented pleasure. God gave it to the human race. The devil only taught us how to misuse it; he adulterated pleasure with evil, making it sinful pleasure. But the fact that some abuse pleasure is no reason for the people of God to abandon it—leaving the impression that pleasure is the devil's concession.

Pleasure, however, must never become lust. Lust is born when pleasure becomes an end in itself, or when pursuing pleasure becomes more important to us than obeying God.

Christians find it hard to hold this truth in balance. It is so much easier to label certain pleasures evil—to say, for example, that sex apart from intended procreation is evil; that movies, novels, dancing, alcohol, tobacco, secular music are taboo; but that playing orchestral arrangements of pretty hymn tunes is virtuous and spiritual. It simplifies the whole question. And on the face of it the approach seems sound. For instance, so much in the movies and on TV is not only garbage but is diabolical garbage.

But we pay a price for such simplistic thinking. If all we were to sacrifice was the enjoyment of God-given delights, the price would be small. However to the degree that we see our faith in negative terms we will, wittingly or unwittingly, so present it. Worse still, whatever we preach to the contrary, we will feel deep down inside us that if we observe the cardinal no-no's, we are being faithful followers of Christ. In fact, our lives may be empty not only of pleasure but also of godliness. Satan will then have gained a major victory in us.

Soldiers in wartime must forego pleasure, not because pleasure is evil (though some pleasures are), but because more pressing claims demand their attention. They may spend bitter months hungry and thirsty, dressed in foul-smelling clothes, with eyes sore with wakefulness, feet blistered and limbs craving rest.

Yet their leaders know the value not only of food and rest but of recreation. They see to it that furloughs are given with an opportunity for the pleasures that have been denied.

Christians are called to warfare. The times we live in will not be normal until Christ returns to reign. Pressing duties demand that we endure hardships and forego pleasure.

Yet at times our heavenly captain will heap upon us not only spiritual delights but, because we have physical bodies, physical delights as well. As followers of Christ, we are not called to pursue pleasure but to follow our leader. Yet we need not be discomfited by the showers of delight he occasionally surprises us with.

Lord, may I not pursue pleasure for its own sake but pursue your goals in the spiritual battle. Yet I thank you for the pleasures you send for my relief and out of your great generosity. Amen.

FOURTEEN. The Prerequisite of Guidance ◊

Trust in the LORD with all your heart . . . and he will make your paths straight.
PROVERBS 3:5-6

I f I had to choose the thing that is most important before a person can know God's will, I would say that yielding everything to God comes first. But I'm afraid that's not number one on God's list. If I am to be guided, I must first *have confidence in God.*

God's whole object is to teach us to walk with him, to teach us to have fellowship with him. When he puts a problem in our way, and we don't know which way to turn, God moves us to enter anew into a relationship of trust with him. Can I really say I believe that Jesus rose from the dead if I can't believe that he will guide me about my everyday affairs? The God who raised Christ is the God who has promised to guide me. So I begin with faith.

Trusting in the Lord is not a feeling. When Solomon says, "Trust in the Lord with all your *heart*," he does not mean emotion or conscience, but will. Trust is a decision. It is coming to God and saying, "Lord, I don't see how you are going to guide me, but I choose to believe that you're going to. I'm going to look to you and you alone for guidance. You are more concerned about this problem than I am. So I have decided to base my future actions on that confidence."

Picture an Eskimo who comes to Winnipeg and sees skyscrapers for the first time. You tell him, "Press that button, and you'll go to the fifteenth floor." His feelings may not tell him that he will go to the fifteenth floor. But if he trusts you and presses the button, it will happen. In the same way, we first trust God (which includes obeying him) and then see his guidance in our lives.

I desire your guidance, Lord. Help me to focus first, rather than on circumstances and feelings, on trusting in you. Amen.

FIFTEEN. Love Is a Hunger ◊

Taste and see that the LORD is good.
PSALM 34:8

L ove is a hunger, and hunger can be suppressed. If you were to ask me during the hours and days when I keep my appetite at bay so I can devote myself to other compelling matters, "Aren't you hungry?" I would answer, "No, I don't think so. No—not in the least." Yet place me in a chair, serve me a good meal and sit down to eat with me. Out of politeness I will arrange my napkin and begin to stick my fork in a piece of meat. And once the smell and the taste of the food assail my senses I will say, "My, that tastes good! Know what? I am hungry!"

So it is with love for God. It lies within many of us like a coiled spring, inactive but straining for release. It is a potential volcano, a dangerous thing that we fear to set free lest in failing to assuage it we shall have to cope with raging fire.

How we fear passion! Yet how great is our need to warm the cold mechanics of our daily routine at her fires! And who can guarantee that released longings will not lead to pain? I cannot.

> Deep calls to deep
> in the roar of your waterfalls;
> All your waves and breakers
> have swept over me.
>
> I say to God my Rock,
> "Why have you forgotten me?
> Why must I go about mourning,
> oppressed by the enemy?"
>
> My bones suffer mortal agony
> as my foes taunt me,
> saying to me all day long,
> "Where is your God?" (Ps 42:7, 9-10)

Our problem is not a want of yearning but a fear of releasing yearning from the grave where we have buried it. But unless we take the risk of loving, we will only be half alive. We belong among the living, not among the dead. Do not be afraid of the longing within; it is more than matched by the greater longing of a God who planted it there. He waits for our response and is not satisfied with our feeble prayer talk. He wants to know us intimately and to disclose to us the secrets of his heart.

Come, then, for love's sake. Come boldly defying fears. Enter into a love-pact to meet Christ daily. Come trembling to confess inadequacies. He is gentle and will understand. He will not force us or hurry the pace beyond what we are able to tolerate.

Come to his footstool. Come trusting. And come for love of him.

Lord Christ, I want take this risk of loving. These deep yearnings—I know they can be filled only by you. I come trembling. But I will trust you, who made me, to love me well. Then, please teach me to love you well in return. Amen.

SIXTEEN. A Glorious Fear ◊

Now let the fear of the LORD be upon you.
2 CHRONICLES 19:7

F inite, sinful men and women may feel fear in the presence of a holy God. God's holiness is ultimate moral beauty, moral beauty of such a nature and such power that it transcends human understanding. It is the living God himself.

I have felt such a fear. I have trembled, perspired, known my muscles turn to water. On one occasion it was as I prayed with elders and deacons in my home. I had tried to teach them what worship was, but I doubt that on that occasion they understood. We then turned to prayer. Perhaps partly to be a model to them I began to express worship, conscious of the poverty of my words.

Then suddenly I saw in front of me a column of flame of about two feet in width. It seemed to arise from beneath the floor and to pass through the ceiling of the room. I knew—without being told—knew by some infallible kind of knowing that transcended the use of my intellect, that I was in the presence of the God of holiness. In stunned amazement I watched a rising column of flames in our living room, while my brothers remained with heads quietly bowed and their eyes closed.

Did they know what was happening? They made no comment afterward and I never asked them. In some obscure fashion I felt I was in the presence of reality and that my brothers were asleep. For years afterward I never spoke of the incident. The others who were present could not have perceived the blend of stark terror and joy that threatened to sweep me away. How could I live and see what I saw? Garbled words of love and of worship tumbled out of my mouth as I struggled to hang on to my self-control. I was no longer trying to worship. Worship was undoing me, pulling me apart. And to be pulled apart was both terrifying and full of glory.

Lord of Glory, reveal to me as much of yourself as I need to see. May I now fear experiencing the glorious fear of your presence. Amen.

SEVENTEEN. Strong Faith ◊

Be strong in the Lord and in the strength of his might.
EPHESIANS 6:10 RSV

S trong faith is faith that continues to respond to the Word of God in the absence of outward encouragement. It is the faith of my little dog who sits obediently on the lawn when we go off shopping in the car and is still waiting for us when we return. It is the church's refusal to abandon the hope of Christ's return in spite of the fact that in the first century and in the thirteenth century every indication might have pointed then to his soon return. But he didn't come. He said he would come soon. That was two thousand years ago.

I am talking about Abraham—old, dried-up Abraham—hobbling to the altar with his strapping manly son and lifting his knife to kill the boy as a sacrifice, believing that the promise made years before would still be fulfilled through this same Isaac, however crazy God's immediate instructions might seem.

I am talking about what appears to observers as a smiling insanity, yet what is in fact a glorious gamble with a clear-eyed perception both of what the odds appear to be on the surface and of what they really are.

I am talking of Paul singing with Silas in jail at midnight or wind-whipped on the deck of a storm-battered ship calming the panicky crew with an assurance that all would be well. These all exemplify an irrevocable commitment, not only to principles, but to the Word of God—come drought, come tornado, come ten feet of snow. This, this ability not to quit obeying no matter what may seem to go wrong, this is strong faith. To grow in your capacity to persist like this is to increase your faith.

Lord of all circumstances, I don't see much, but I believe. When life doesn't go the way I want, when doubts boil within me, when I don't feel like believing, still I believe—not because I am strong, but because you are strong. Amen.

EIGHTEEN. What the Spirit Helps Us to See ◊

When he, the Spirit of truth, comes, he will guide you into all truth.
JOHN 16:13

Years ago in a daily prayer meeting, missionary prayer-letter files were passed around. One morning my file contained a letter from a missionary in the Philippines. In it she described her hospitalization in Manila for spinal tuberculosis. Her condition was serious and at the time called for a prolonged period in a sanatorium in a body cast. Unexpectedly (for the woman was a stranger to me) I was not only profoundly shaken but found myself virtually insisting that God heal her right away.

My prayer was remarkable in that I did not believe such healing was possible, and so I was astounded by both the content and the urgency of my own prayer. I suppose you could say that the Holy Spirit was allowing me to "see" two realities—the need of the young missionary, and God's power to do something my theology and medical experience told me was impossible. To the astonishment of her physician, this woman in the Philippines was miraculously healed that same day and soon after became my wife.

The Holy Spirit's illumination will vary in its intensity and degree. At times we will not feel it at all. But it must always be sought. And it will operate not by a direct operation on our feelings so much as by the illumination of our inner vision to reality. God wants us to share his concerns and be caught up into his purposes. Of course our absence of feeling can mean we no longer care about the things of God. We have grown lukewarm—a temperature God detests. In that case we are called on to confess our sin and to repent of our lack of devotion to his person. He will meet us, cleanse us and renew us when we do.

I praise you, Lord, that you prompt me to pray, and that you answer by doing the impossible. Help me to be responsive when my inner vision perceives your reality— and able to trust when it does not. Amen.

NINETEEN. Tempted ◊

One evening David got up from his bed and walked around on the roof of the palace.

2 SAMUEL 11:2

David's affair with Bathsheba shows a treacherous side to his nature. Power had corrupted him.

His decision to entrust war to his generals may have been a matter of laziness. His idle wandering on the rooftop after a late afternoon nap during a time of war is inconsistent with his responsibilities. His voyeurism and lust for Bathsheba show his weakness as a man and his abuse of prerogatives as a king. He saw her, he lusted after her and he ordered her to come to the palace. You will find the whole story in 2 Samuel 11.

Perhaps Bathsheba is not without blame. Did she realize she could be observed as she bathed in the garden? Did she perhaps wish to be observed? We do not know. If she were innocent of exhibitionism, the invitation to the royal bed would put her in an awkward position. Yet it takes two to commit adultery, royal or otherwise, and Bathsheba showed no resistance.

According to God's law for Israel David had already committed two sins, one of which carried a death sentence. He had simultaneously lain with a woman during her "impurity" and committed adultery. The king should be the first to keep the law, but the king had broken it. Had he been leading his army, the incident would never have occurred.

The lesson for us is plain. If we are doing *what* we should *when* we should, we shall be less exposed to temptation.

Father, sometimes I like to play a little with temptation before I put it in its place. Help me to remember, when it first appears, how dangerous that is. Help me to flee it, not flirt with it. Amen.

TWENTY. Where Is the Battle? ◊

Put on the full armor of God so you can take your stand against the devil's schemes.
EPHESIANS 6:11

During World War 2 when bombs rained ruin from the skies on Britain, some self-styled experts argued fiercely about the precise manner in which the war would end, endlessly debating the fate of the Italians, the role of the Americans in Italy, in France, scheduling and rescheduling the order of events. These Britons argued huddled inside bomb shelters while London burned.

Other Britons wore helmets to protect their heads from the hot, jagged shrapnel that fell like hailstones, dug among the rubble of ruined homes and factories, dragged men and women from burning ruins, drove ambulances. Yet others looked through gun sights as they patrolled the city or flew tiny fighter planes below the stars, looking for incoming bombs to shoot out of the air.

Some talked. Some fought. Doubtless the experts in the shelters felt in some obscure way that the war was in their hands. Psychologically they needed to feel in control and their talk, their pseudoexpertise, gave them the security that bomb shelters alone could not provide. Meanwhile the real war was going on where shrapnel fell and bombs exploded.

It is so today. We are called on to fight, not to be experts on the end times. We are called to bear witness in life or death to the King of glory.

May I be among those, Lord, who fight for your righteous cause. Amen.

TWENTY-ONE. The God of Love and Anger ◊

But who can endure the day of his coming? Who can stand when he appears? For he will be like a refiner's fire.
MALACHI 3:2

There is no room for doubt. From Genesis to Revelation our God is a God of anger.

How, then, do we see God's anger in relation to his other attributes? Does he stop loving when he gets angry? Where do his gentleness and longsuffering go? You know the answers. God is loving *as well as* angry. He is patient and longsuffering *as well as* enraged.

In fact, God never *becomes* angry. He is, was and will be eternally angry. He is angry with evil and sin. He does not *begin to be* angry with us. It is better to say that when we do evil we walk into that region where his anger already exists, eternally the same.

God's love clearly is more basic than his anger. Scripture says that God is love, yet we never read that God is anger. We might say that his anger arises out of his love. Love and anger come together at Calvary.

You see, anger is the measure of love. Even here on earth we can see that. A normal man is terribly hurt and angry if his wife is unfaithful. If this hurt and angry man loves his wife enough to accept her back, to forgive her and treat her tenderly, then we know he really loves her. On the other hand, if he just shrugs his shoulders at her adultery, we can be pretty sure he doesn't care for her at all. In fact, a man who is never angry is a feeble, shallow, selfish kind of man. He confuses love with emotional goo.

I'm all for an angry God. Not just because I love him and trust him, but because of what I see in the world around me. Would you want a God who could overlook today's terrorism? The holocausts of concentration camps? The exploitation by commercial enterprises of starving people? The Gulag Archipelago?

His wrath was on Egypt, Assyria, Babylonia, on sinning Israel and

Judah. His wrath burns on against iniquity: crime against elderly people in our cities, the persecution of his saints under repressive governments, all of the world's torture chambers—everything that exalts itself against him and all he stands for.

So we must be careful not to think that there is something contradictory about a loving God being angry. God is angry over injustice. He is angry about human suffering and the sin that causes it. He is angry with you when you sin. And the heat of his anger with you is the measure of his love for you. If you reject the idea of his anger, it is because you find his love interferes too much in your personal affairs.

Lord God, I tremble at your anger; I thrill at your forgiving love. Thank you that the one does not cancel the other out. Amen.

TWENTY-TWO. Eliminating Stress ◊

I do not have time to tell about Gideon, Barak, Samson, Jephthah, David, Samuel and the prophets, who through faith conquered kingdoms, administered justice, and gained what was promised; who shut the mouths of lions, quenched the fury of the flames, and escaped the edge of the sword; whose weakness was turned to strength; and who became powerful in battle and routed foreign armies.

HEBREWS 11:32-34

Stress is recognized to be the cause of many major diseases. Popular books warn us of its dangers and teach us how to avoid it or, failing that, how to cope with it when it arises.

From all over the Western world, where Christians enjoy liberty and prosperity, I receive letters requesting seminars on eliminating stress. The letters trouble me. They stand in contrast to letters from some Third-World countries where Christians are persecuted and thus under tremendous stress. From these countries come letters requesting instruction on faithfulness and on the cost of discipleship.

By and large, Third-World Christians take stress for granted. When they are not struggling merely to survive, their joy in the kingdom seems to make them indifferent to the cost of kingdom service. It may be that while we in the West live in an artificially secure environment our brothers and sisters have a better chance of seeing life as it really is. Eternity is a little closer to them. When the skulls of starvation grin at you, when danger makes life a day-by-day affair, when there is no technology to buffer the crudities of life, one has different values—values less inimical to Christ's rule in our hearts.

Following Christ may actually involve us in more stress rather than less. The call to follow is a call to advance from stress to stress. Happily it is also a call to go from strength to strength.

We are mistaken when we suppose that stress is an evil that must be avoided at all costs. The same stress that kills can also make us tougher, stronger, more resilient.

During World War 2, British prime minister Winston Churchill was under ceaseless stress, working constantly, sleeping little, bearing crushing responsibilities. His country could have been invaded at any moment. Only twenty-two miles of sea separated him from the greatest evil power on earth. Yet his personality blossomed. He thrived on the experience. This can be true for us, when we are working in obedience to God.

I ask, Lord, not that you would eliminate stress from my life but that you would give me the grace to meet each problem and a heart that is faithful to you even when hard times come. Amen.

TWENTY-THREE. Reconciliation with Others ◊

If we walk in the light, as he is in the light, we have fellowship with one another.

1 JOHN 1:7

A s Christians we all hold in common the fruits of our reconciliation with God. These touch the raw depths of our souls, our deepest fears, our blackest guilts. Divine love has met us to cover our secret shame, to abolish our guilt and to remove our fears in an ongoing, forgiving and caring relationship.

But divine love places us under an obligation. Cleansing must continue. We must love as we have been loved, accept as we have been accepted, forgive as we have been forgiven. The task is not easy.

Ken Blue once counseled two sisters, both members of the same church, who had been quarreling since their childhood. When he called them together he found they had so many grievances that they hardly knew where to begin. Eventually each sister aired her complaints while Ken sat and listened. But before long the meeting degenerated into a shouting match. Ken intervened to point out that the object of the exercise, according to Jesus, was reconciliation. But reconciliation was the furthest thing from both sisters' minds.

Ken knew, however, that both sisters genuinely loved Christ and were committed to obedience. He therefore made a second approach, going to each sister privately and telling each that to refuse reconciliation with the other would be treason against her Lord. There was a second meeting where deep reconciliation was sealed. More importantly, the reconciliation has held up. Each sister's tenderness for Christ won out.

We struggle. Our faith at times wanes unaccountably. To our shame, we fall repeatedly into sin, hopefully to find renewed forgiveness and deliverance. And these experiences too are to be offered to and shared with those who are in need. To share in "the fellowship of the saints" is to belong to a reconciled and reconciling community, bound together by bonds of loving faithfulness.

Lord Jesus Christ, thank you for what the fellowship of the saints means in the most ordinary of relationships. Thank you for the miracle of a group of people living as your church in this world and helping others see who you are. I do not always participate in this miracle. Help me please to forgive as I have been forgiven, and to be a reconciler. Amen.

TWENTY-FOUR. Guilty ◊

But when the kindness and love of God our Savior appeared, he saved us . . . so that, having been justified by his grace, we might become heirs having the hope of eternal life. This is a trustworthy saying.

TITUS 3:4-8

Religious patients especially are plagued with feelings of guilt. Their knowledge of God's grace and mercy seems powerless to help them. They condemn themselves as lazy, as bad parents, as ungrateful spouses, as poor providers, as bad witnesses, as self-pitying and the like. They may "understand" the nature of God's forgiveness but lack any sense of it. Told to trust facts and not feelings, they struggle to obey but sometimes their troubled minds embrace ideas they have long resisted. They decide that they never were Christians or that they have committed the unpardonable sin. "All my friends tell me I'm a Christian," said a bewildered little lady the other day, "and I used to think I was myself. But I know now that I'm not."

This crippling sense of guilt often arises from an inadequate grasp of the grace of God in the face of Satanic accusations (see Rev 12:10-11). Much evangelical teaching renders Christians peculiarly vulnerable to it. No one ever says so explicitly but most evangelicals, I am convinced, unconsciously assume that God's loving acceptance of them depends on their postconversion spiritual performance rather than on the perfect sacrifice on their behalf by the Son of man. They know the theory of justification but derive no spiritual succor from it.

It is impossible to exaggerate the crippling paralysis caused by an inadequate understanding of God's justifying grace. Likewise, is it impossible to exaggerate the joy and gratitude that can overwhelm those who have understood and experienced the freedom of God's grace.

Jesus, I look into your eyes as you hang there on the cross, and I see you looking back into my eyes and saying to me, "I'm glad I can do this for you." I am overwhelmed. Thank you, Jesus. Amen.

TWENTY-FIVE. Freedom through Slavery ◊

If anyone would come after me, he must deny himself and take up his cross daily and follow me.

LUKE 9:23

To be free means to be released from being torn in two directions at once. It means to have one passion only—one pearl of great price—rather than half a dozen conflicting passions.

Let me quote to you a letter written some years ago by an American Communist in Mexico City, a letter breaking his engagement with his fiancée.

We communists suffer many casualties. We are those whom they shoot, hang, lynch, tar and feather, imprison, slander, fire from our jobs and whose lives people make miserable in every way possible. Some of us are killed and imprisoned. We live in poverty. From what we earn we turn over to the Party every cent which we do not absolutely need to live.

We communists have neither time nor money to go to movies very often, nor for concerts nor for beautiful homes and new cars. They call us fanatics. We are fanatics. Our lives are dominated by one supreme factor—the struggle for world communism. We communists have a philosophy of life that money could not buy. We have a cause to fight for, a specific goal in life. We lose our insignificant identities in the great river of humanity; and if our personal lives seem hard or if our egos seem bruised through subordination to the Party, we are amply rewarded—in the thought that all of us, even though it be in a very small way, are contributing something new and better for humanity.

There is one thing about which I am completely in earnest—the communist cause. It is my life, my business, my religion, my hobby, my sweetheart, my wife, my mistress, my meat and drink. I work at it by day and dream of it by night. Its control over me grows greater with the passage of time. Therefore I cannot have a friend, a lover or even a conversation without relating them to this power that animates and controls my life. I measure people, books, ideas and deeds according to the way they affect the communist cause and by their attitude to it. I have already been in jail for my ideas, and if need be I am ready to face death.

If the letter fails to stir you, you may already have begun to die. Like a traveler lost in a blizzard, unaware your body freezes in a snow bank, you are drifting to sleep. But if your heart beats more quickly—be glad. You have hope of a more bracing life than the one most of us live.

The unknown Communist in Mexico City startles us into seeing how trivial our lives are. We may not share his opinions. But we may sense that he has been set free from lesser passions by the pursuit of greater ones. Christ offers us greater passions still. For he did not call us to suburbia and a mortgage but to a gallows and a crown of glory.

Renew, rekindle, revive in me the fire of desire to follow you wherever you go, Lord. Grant me a single-minded commitment to your way, your truth and your life. Amen.

TWENTY-SIX. The Priorities in Guidance ◊

Whoever finds his life will lose it, and whoever loses his life for my sake will find it.

MATTHEW 10:39

God is not interested in guiding us about just one choice. His priority is much larger than that.

Suppose I say to an interior decorator, "Look at our dining room. It's a mess. Please do something about it."

But the interior decorator might respond, "Your dining room is a mess. But the problem is that your whole house is a mess. I can't fix the dining room without also dealing with everything that is around it. Give me the whole house to decorate and I'll do the job. But don't ask me to do the dining room alone."

When we come to God asking for guidance, he says, "Give me your life." This is his priority. He does not want to guide us about a specific issue alone. "You have that problem in your life," he says, "because you have not given me the whole of your life. It's not that I can't solve this problem in isolation. It's that the trouble extends to the whole of your life. I want to give your whole life its proper orientation."

He doesn't say this because he is unsympathetic. He cares deeply. Toward the end of *The Magician's Nephew*, Digory is confronted by Aslan.

"Son of Adam," said Aslan. "Are you ready to undo the wrong you have done to my sweet country of Narnia?" . . .

"Yes," said Digory. . . . "But please, please—won't you—can't you give me something that will cure my Mother?" Up till then he had been looking at the Lion's great front feet and the huge claws on them; now, in his despair, he looked up at its face. What he saw surprised him as much as anything in his whole life. For the tawny face was bent down near his own and (wonder of wonders) great shining tears stood in the Lion's eyes. They were such big, bright tears compared with Digory's own that for a moment he felt as if the Lion must really be sorrier about his Mother than he was himself.

We may feel that God doesn't care about our problems, but his heart knows more sorrow than we could ever know. For this very reason he wants to give us the best in all aspects of our being. Following Christ is a lifetime occupation. It's not just going to church and perhaps having a time when you read your Bible each day. *Let him lead all that you do.*

Lord, I want to follow your priorities. Help me to see beyond the present situation for which I need guidance; enable me to lift my whole life to you (and not snatch it back). Thank you. Amen.

TWENTY-SEVEN. A Quiet Spirit ◊

[Your beauty] should be that of your inner self, the unfading beauty of a gentle and quiet spirit, which is of great worth in God's sight.
1 PETER 3:4

If you were to take a mild tranquilizer half an hour before a family explosion, you might exude peace when it happened. Your anxieties would lessen, leaving you serene and gentle. Inner worries would seem trivial. Conflict in the family would frighten you less, and you could approach problems calmly as long as the pill lasted. Sensing this (and provided you hadn't taken too much), tension would begin to subside in the rest of the family—but at the cost of exposing you to a bad and dangerous habit.

I do not recommend tranquilizers for family conflicts. You need a genuine peace, the kind that makes dogs wag their tails and babies hold out their arms to you. Nor is the peace I recommend an "oh-it-doesn't-matter" peace, a peace that lets vital matters slide or that fails to come to grips with family problems. It must condone neither irresponsibility nor escapism but must be a peace arising from an inner assurance that all is well—the clear-eyed peace of a person who is in touch with God.

When you are upset, irritated, angry, you cannot contribute to peace in others. But when your spirit is quiet and at rest, then when you intervene in a hassle your peace will reassure others, diminishing their resentment. Move in with a belligerent attitude and you may succeed in controlling expressions of hostility in your family, but you will never solve the resentments and bitterness that gave rise to the storm in the first place. A meek and a quiet spirit is of great price in God's sight and an equally priceless resource in family life.

When dinner blows up and the car breaks down and my family can't seem to have a civilized conversation, grant to me, Lord, the inner peace of knowing you. Put today's troubles in your eternal perspective. Grant me your peace, O Lord. Amen.

TWENTY-EIGHT. The Risk of Spiritual Power ◊

Do not rejoice that the spirits submit to you, but rejoice that your names are written in heaven.
LUKE 10:20

The same atomic power that lights a city and fuels its industries can annihilate a city when it gets out of control. Chernobyl is a repeatable nightmare. The power under the hood of an ordinary automobile can kill and maim. Power always can be wrongly used.

Spiritual power is no exception to the rule. God "took the risk" (though that is not the best way to express the matter, for he knew exactly what he was doing and what would follow) of giving plenty of it to Satan and the hosts of angels who rebelled. They absconded with the power he had bestowed on them and catastrophe followed. A cosmic war began that still continues. God even bestows power on fallible, immature human beings when he makes them his partners in the gospel. He has yet to invent a dangerproof power.

Divine power is holy power. People entrusted with it carry a heavy burden of responsibility. Those who reverence its source and realize the responsibility that comes with it, respect it. Others have exercised divine power and have displeased God by the way they did so. Jesus told his disciples, "Many will say to me on that day, 'Lord, Lord, did we not prophesy in your name, and in your name drive out demons and perform many miracles?' Then will I tell them plainly, 'I never knew you. Away from me, you evildoers!' " (Mt 7:22-23).

I do not understand why God gives more power to other people than he does to me. I resent it at times. But God has his own reasons, and my resentment is out of place. He is God and he knows what he is doing. Any of us can mishandle any gracious gift he bestows on us. Yet he never ceases to bestow.

Being sinful and weak, we can be clumsy in handling power and get into difficulties. But God does not take the same risks with us that the sorcerer took with his legendary apprentice. His purposes will never be frustrated, nor will his plans suffer from our bungling. But *we* may.

Powerful God, make me ready before you bestow your power on me, so that I may not dishonor you or hurt your people or your work by using it wrongly. Meanwhile, enable me to serve you in more ordinary ways without envy or grumbling. Amen.

TWENTY-NINE. Family ◊

I bow my knees before the Father, from whom every family in heaven and on earth is named.
EPHESIANS 3:14-15 RSV

T he family, however much we may wish to change it, remains at its healthiest only when its members relate as God designed them to relate. It was designed to function neither as a democracy nor as a dictatorship nor yet as an economic unit in an agrarian society. Social change may modify its size or its links with the rest of the world, but nothing has and nothing ever will alter its essential nature.

Families exist because God designed humans to live in families. And whatever futurologists may say to the contrary, the moment we cease to live *en famille* we will cease to be distinctly human, will become more antlike. I make this statement on biblical rather than scientific grounds. All science can say (whether the science of anthropology, sociology or psychology) is what *is* happening to families and what *might* happen to them. Science can never say what *ought* to happen since science has no way of knowing what a *normal* family is. It can only know what a *usual* family *seems* to be like in a given cultural setting. Normality lies beyond the bailiwick of science. It implies purpose and design of which science knows nothing.

God is not a bachelor; he is a Trinity.

Whatever way we may conceive or fail to conceive the nature of the Trinity, of one thing we may be sure. Human beings did not invent it out of their neurotic need for security. People who say that *humans* created *God* as a father forget this. God, as he is revealed to us, comes not just as Father, but as a Three-in-One, an entity which we cannot understand let alone invent.

However, he *is* revealed to us as Father; and humans, created in his image, are created also with an innate capacity for intimate personal relationships. The family unit may well meet basic biological needs. It may correlate with certain cultural and economic conditions, but these needs and conditions are less basic than we suppose. The family unit arises out of *what God is* in the very core of his being.

I thank you that families are part of your plan, Father—that they fit with who you are. I thank you that through your Son I can be part of your eternal family, here on earth and forever in heaven. Amen.

THIRTY. Worshiping with the Wise Men ◊

On coming to the house, [the Magi] saw the child with his mother Mary, and they bowed down and worshiped him.
MATTHEW 2:11

In spirit I go with the Wise Men and the shepherds to look and wonder. I see a baby that looks much like any other baby. No halo, no beautiful smile (newborn babies do not smile). No frills or talcum powder either. Just a baby in the swaddling clothes of a peasant. When it is hungry it screws up its little face and cries (I shrink from saying "*He* screws up *his* face and cries"). It has to be fed.

I fall down with the Wise Men and worship. I worship not only because I am in the presence of God but because I am beginning for the first time to see what God is like. And I am overwhelmed. I want to turn my head away for I am appalled at his humiliation. And yet I want to look, for I am glad with all my heart that he has done it. He has become one of us. He has not despised the virgin's womb. He has been born of a woman, made under the Law. He has come to live among us, to suffer and to die. So I worship. And with my cracked voice, as well as I can, I sing with the heavenly host who adore him: Glory to God in the highest. Oh, come let us adore him, Christ the Lord.

Jesus, my mind recoils from the facts of your coming into such demeaned human circumstances. But my heart swells with joy at what that coming meant. Thanks be to you, glorious Lord Christ. Amen.

MONTH
THREE

ONE. No Excuses ◊

*Against you, you only, have I sinned and done what is evil in your sight.
. . . Surely I was sinful at birth, sinful from the time my mother conceived me.*

PSALM 51:4-5

Your sinfulness is never an excuse for your sin. You have, it is true, a fallen nature. Like Paul, you groan that mortality might be clothed with immortality. But wretched person that you are, sin overwhelms you. You do not know how you will ever overcome your weaknesses. It is important that you acknowledge this, not as an excuse, but as a recognition of your utter sinfulness.

The acknowledgment must not be one of self-pity. It will not do to say, "I'm no good anyway. I'm totally rotten and I never will be able to quit sinning." Don't be so petulant. You must not blame God, which is exactly what you do when you talk like this. You are bitter because you do not like what you see. And so long as you remain bitter and resentful, so long as you cannot accept yourself without resentment, you do not *confess* what you are to God; you only *complain* about it. Complaints never lead to healing. Confession does.

You may say, "How can I be responsible for what I am when other people made me what I am?" Theologians differ in the kinds of answers they supply to this question. Perhaps a simple illustration will help to make the idea more acceptable.

Let us suppose that you inherit from your father a large estate but that there are many debts against the estate. You talk it over and think that with energy and with new ideas you can clear up the financial difficulties. But you fail. You fail partly because you are not as hardworking or skillful as you thought you were and partly because you began with certain odds against you.

Now you could say, "It's not my fault. If my father had not made such a mess of things I would not be in this position today."

Yet you *are* in that position. Your excuse will not interest your creditors. It is irrelevant. To blame your father may help your bruised ego but it will not change things. You have no choice but to accept the responsibility of your debts. As a matter of fact, whether you are faced with bankruptcy or some totally different problem, the only attitude which will allow you peace of mind, indeed the only mature attitude, will be, "I may as well face the fact that I'm in a hopeless position. Excuses won't help. I'll just have to face the music myself."

In the same way, face the fact of your sin squarely. Let down your defenses. Then God can help you.

All right, Lord, I will no longer make excuses. I will own my part in the dysfunction of my life. Please forgive me for sinning against you. Help me see where I can make amends; then enable me to hand this sin over to you for the cleansing you have provided in the blood of Christ. Amen.

TWO. What Are We, Anyway? ◊

I praise you because I am fearfully and wonderfully made.
PSALM 139:14

What is a human being? A complex bundle of neuron pathways, says the reflexologist. Jab people with a pin and they jump. Freeze them and they bundle themselves up with clothing and build a fire. Deep inside our amazing brains are chemical memory patterns that tell us that these are the appropriate ways to react to pain and cold. We don't really "think" (though we *think* we "think"). We don't "decide" either. Everything we do is predetermined by stimuli from the environment acting on the complex chemistry of our central nervous systems. "Will," "mind" and even "consciousness" are illusions.

What is a human being? A mass of statistical data, says the statistician. Several million are starving. Several million others eat too much. The figures for both groups are exploding. But the trends are fascinating, and we've made great progress in our understanding of humanity since the advent of the computer.

What is a human being? The highest of the mammals, says the zoologist. A social animal, declares the anthropologist. The suffering victim of social and family pressures, affirms the psychoanalyst. A victim of the class struggle, says Marx.

So there you have us—dissected, computerized, reduced to a mass of nervous pathways and overwhelming statistics. But the Bible offers a different picture of us, more different than these explanations are from each other. They have defined us from our behavior; the Bible goes right to our essence. It says we are made in the image of God. The Bible reveals things about humankind that science will never discover. We can only quarrel with those who say "We are this *and nothing more.*" For we are more. Having described our physiology, we are a long way from having said what is most important about us. What the Bible has to say is key. For we can be described not only in terms of the physical universe but also in terms of eternal purpose.

Creator God, unless you give me meaning and a heart to perceive it, I am only a machine or an animal. Thank you for letting me know something of your definition of a human being. Amen.

THREE. What Are We Made For? ◊

From the lips of children and infants you have ordained praise.
PSALM 8:2

If we want to know what anything *is,* we must ask *what it is for.* What is a bread knife? You could say it is a thin strip of steel, sharpened along one edge, and your statement would be accurate. But if you said nothing more, you'd have said very little. If, on the other hand, you said that a bread knife is something you cut bread with, you'd be getting nearer the heart of the matter.

Therefore, our understanding of humanity will be at best sadly incomplete unless we see what we are for. At this point the Bible can give us only part of the answer, since our minds cannot stretch enough to grasp the whole. Among other things, we were created *to enjoy God by knowing him.* "Let him who boasts boast about this: that he understands and knows me, that I am the LORD" (Jer 9:24). We were also made *to please him by knowing him.* "I desire . . . acknowledgment of God rather than burnt offerings" (Hos 6:6).

To know him and enjoy him we must in some respects be like him, and have something in us that corresponds to him. Wonderfully, this is not merely a vain longing. We were made in his image—responsible, moral beings (Gen 1:26-27; Ps 8:4-9). If this is so, and if our end is to know God—how great is human dignity! We are more noble than a mere mass of protoplasm, more important than the political creeds we invent, greater than the history we make.

Think of it. We are created to glorify the One who is the God of all time and space.

God of eternity, God of the infinite reaches of space, why do you bother to let me know you and enjoy you? Still, this pleases you, and it gives meaning to my life and warmth to my soul. Thank you. Amen.

FOUR. Riches through Prayer ◊

Buy from me gold refined in fire, so you can become rich.
REVELATION 3:18

When crisis arises in the life of someone we are praying for, it may try us as Christians far more than it would try an unbeliever. For the crisis may challenge all I believe about God. It may seem to give the lie to the very things I have entrusted to God. With a sinking heart I am tempted to think that my prayers have all been self-deception.

It is important when your faith is badly shaken to wait until you have time to spend alone with God before you allow yourself to wallow in despair. And when you do come to God, the first thing you must remember is that he does not mock his children. He is still there. His faithfulness has not wavered a scrap. You may or you may not have misunderstood his will and his intentions about one detail or another. But your mistake, if indeed it is a mistake, does not alter the basic situation.

In your own pain and tragedy you are being invited to enter into a close relationship with God. Whatever may or may not happen to your children, great good and enormous enrichment can come into your own life if only you will draw near to God. You may not enjoy unusual experiences or glory in visions, but your spirit can be set free. You can pass through fire and come out as fine gold. You can become more truly alive, more aware. Your very pain brings with it the possibility of untold riches.

Lord God, I ask not for great visions or miraculous gifts but for your presence near me, the treasure of your love. Amen.

FIVE. Truly Free ◊

Come to me, all you who are weary and burdened, and I will give you rest. Take my yoke upon you and learn from me, for I am gentle and humble in heart, and you will find rest for your souls. For my yoke is easy and my burden is light.

MATTHEW 11:28-30

L et me say a very important thing about freedom: *Freedom does not consist in doing what I want to do but in doing what I was designed to do.* If I do what I want to do, I wind up not liking what I do. What at first promises liberty turns out to be a more onerous slavery.

You fling yourself with wild abandon to serve an ideology, and at first it feels like the most heady liberty you have ever known. But the high subsides. The sense of liberty goes. In the end, the grim, dreary enslavement seems no better than the enslavement to your former selfish whims.

Many Christians find themselves enslaved to a hideous mixture of dogma, spiritual cliché and psychological technique. They are chained to a semi-Christian ideology rather than to a Person.

Do not misunderstand me. I do not underestimate the importance of truth. It is just that humanity was not designed to serve a theory—even a true theory. Theories enslave.

The truth is a Person. Jesus alone gives freedom to human beings. He knows what he designed our beings for. He knows where true freedom exists for us. And he has infinite patience in teaching us, lesson by lesson, how to be free.

Truth can be true but still cold, Lord. But you are a vibrant, living Person to whom I owe my life and loyalty. Thank you for the warmth of your commitment to me, which makes possible my commitment to you. Amen.

SIX. Beyond Mere Geography ◊

Leave your country, your people and your father's household and go to the land I will show you.
GENESIS 12:1

Abraham knew the direction but not the destination. Yet that was sufficient.

We too can know the direction—holiness. God desires to make us holy. But he will not tell us the details. He will not tell us where we will wind up. We have to trust him for that. The question of guidance is a question of faith.

Guidance, you see, is not merely geographical (shall I choose this direction or that?); it is also moral. What is the *right* thing, the upright thing, the godly thing, to do in these circumstances? Admittedly, it is not always easy to *do* what is right just because I *know* what is right. But I will at least know what choice God wants me to make. That is why Psalm 119:9-11 says, "How can a young man keep his way pure? By living according to your word. . . . I have hidden your word in my heart that I might not sin against you." Some think that missionaries are special people. Missionaries know where they're going in life. After all, they're called to a specific country. But you ask missionaries and most will tell you that it is not like that at all. They may have headed for one country and wound up in another. They may have thought of one kind of work and ended up doing something entirely different. All of us have the same kind of guidance; all of us are supposed to have a call in life like Abraham's.

Isaiah 30:21 makes the same point. God says to Israel, "Whether you turn to the right or to the left, your ears will hear a voice behind you, saying, 'This is the way; walk in it.' " Here God is not primarily concerned with geographical guidance or with people learning to do his will. The context of the verse is the moral confusion in Israel: Israel had become idolatrous. The people had been told that there was no inconsistency in worshiping idols and worshiping God. They did not know right from wrong. So God promises them a new teacher, God the Holy Spirit, who will teach them what is right in worship.

The people of Israel found comfort in God's promise to guide them into purity. God wants the same for us. He is not concerned that we win a lottery or even that we avoid all pain. But he is concerned that we find wholeness of life—which can only come through him and in accordance with his ways. And we will find comfort in the new and intimate relationship with a Person who is *the* guide in our life, whose walk with us will mean more than anything else in life.

Be my guide, loving Lord. I know your ways for me are good. Do what is needed to make me holy . . . and whole. Amen.

SEVEN. Have We Shrunk God? ◊

When I saw him, I fell at his feet as though dead.
REVELATION 1:17

E arlier in this century God was under attack. The time came when he was briefly reported to be dead. But during the past half-century he has in fact been trivialized, packaged for entertainment, presented as a sort of psychological panacea, a heavenly glue to keep happy families together, a celestial slot machine to respond to our whims, a formula for success, a fund raiser for pseudoreligious enterprises, a slick phrase for bumper stickers, and a sort of holy pie and ice cream. How impoverished this all is, how virtually blasphemous when compared to the experiences recorded in Scripture!

When John the apostle, slaving in salt mines on the island of Patmos, caught a vision of the glorified Christ, he fell at his feet as dead, so awesome was the sight.

When the prophet Daniel saw that same glory and heard words of thunder, such terror seized his companions (though they themselves saw nothing) that they fled. As for Daniel, he tells us, "My strength left me; I became a sorry figure of a man, and retained no strength. I heard the sound of his words and, when I did so, I fell prone on the ground in a trance. Suddenly a hand grasped me and pulled me up on to my hands and knees. He said to me, 'Daniel, man greatly beloved, attend to the words I am speaking to you. . . .' When he addressed me, I stood up trembling" (Dan 10:8-12 NEB).

When Job was caught up into the whirlwind to hear the words of God, he said, "I have spoken of great things which I have not understood, things too wonderful for me to know. I knew of thee then only by report, but now I see thee with my own eyes. Therefore . . . I repent in dust and ashes" (Job 42:3-6 NEB).

If God is God, it is important that we know him as he is, not as we recreate him in our imaginations. It is important for us to know him as he is, for how can we speak to others of him when we have never trembled before his glory? Is it not possible that for all our biblical expertise and our claims about the Spirit's power, we still present a God who is small enough to fit inside our tiny brains?

Lord, I try to imagine the greatest power in the universe—a power greater than the universe—and still it is so small compared to your true greatness. May I know more of your glory and power today. Amen.

EIGHT. Lighthouse of Peace ◊

Peace I leave with you; my peace I give you. I do not give to you as the world gives. Do not let your hearts be troubled and do not be afraid.
JOHN 14:27

J esus gave the apostles these words of peace as they were about to face a tumultuous reception in a hostile world. The peace Christ gave them did not shelter them *from* the tumults, accusations or persecution, but it sustained them *in* those circumstances. The Jesus who spoke peace to them was the same Jesus who from a wildly rocking fishing boat had shouted into the teeth of a gale, "Peace! Be still!" bringing its furies to an astonished halt and causing the impassioned waters to lap meekly around the sides of the boat. His word to their hearts was no less effective than his word in the storm. He gave them peace, *his* peace, with which they subsequently strode through demonic storms of raging hatred.

Being the Prince of Peace he could say to them, "I have told you these things, so that in me you may have peace. In this world you will have trouble. But take heart! I have overcome the world" (Jn 16:33). In Christ, peace. In the world, tribulation. But Christ has overcome the world. The peace he spoke of was not a sort of spiritual tranquilizer, sedating the nervous systems of jumpy disciples. It was the peace of a strong man in control. The peace the disciples were to experience *arose from their relationship with him and from his relationship with the world.*

Picture yourself in a well-built lighthouse founded on solid rock. Huge waves might crash and mighty gales might scream around it, yet inside the lighthouse is peace. Out in the storm you would be buffeted, bruised and soaked to the skin. But the lighthouse is overcoming the storm in the same way that Jesus overcomes the world. The rain may dash itself against the walls and the windows but from inside you need have no concern.

Such is the peace Jesus offers that Paul speaks of it as "the peace of God, which passes all understanding" (Phil 4:7 RSV). "Great peace" is the psalmist's description (Ps 119:165).

Jesus, thank you that you are peace and you give peace. In the tumult of my life today, teach me to enter more deeply into your gift of peace. Amen.

NINE. Repeated Prayer ◊

When you pray, do not keep on babbling like pagans, for they think they will be heard because of their many words.

MATTHEW 6:7

You may be tempted to pray repetitively, constantly demanding the same thing over and over again. It is as though by keeping the matter constantly active in your prayers you will make doubly sure that it will not find its way to the bottom of a heap of other people's requests or perhaps be filed by a heavenly clerk into an inactive drawer. It may dismay you perhaps to discover you have forgotten to pray for Jack's sanctification for a whole week and to realize simultaneously that Jack's sanctification now seems much less possible than it did when you first prayed about it. You feel as though you are losing ground in the battle to get the prayer pushed through and begin to agitate so that it gets proper priority.

We are not heard for our many words. God is not a busy executive with too many details to cope with. Yet what should we do once we have prayed and thought matters through? Do we then dismiss them from our minds? How should we regard the requests we have made while we are waiting for them to come to pass?

Certainly we should not forget them. If we entertain no doubts whatever that the requests will come to pass, then we should praise God constantly for what he will do. We praise because God is worthy to be praised and not because praise is a way of exerting pressure on God or of guaranteeing our hopes. Nor do we cease to praise and thank God once our prayers are answered; we must continue to praise him for past answers to prayer. If doubts do arise with the passage of time, we should bring the matter again before God, confessing our doubts and uncertainties asking for more wisdom.

Whatever doubts we may have about God's specific will in a problem, of one thing we should never be in doubt: God will give us wisdom when we ask him. He will meet us, hear us and continue to instruct us as we wait on him. "If any of you lacks wisdom, he should ask God, who gives generously to all without finding fault, and it will be given to him" (Jas 1:5).

Thus we may keep our requests active in our own minds. We do not allow ourselves to forget about our dealings with God. The lessons he teaches us must be kept alive in our daily thoughts so they will not be forgotten and so we will not slip back into old ways of looking at things. We do not keep them active so God will not forget (he neither will nor can) but for our own benefit. In this way we may sometimes find that we were too hasty about some requests whereas our conviction will continue to grow about others.

The number of times we pray for something is not the crucial thing. It is much more important that we exercise faith, that is, that we adopt attitudes of mind and will as we learn to trust God. Faith is not the coin with which we barter for God's blessings. God waits to bestow blessings by sovereign grace, and faith "as a grain of mustard seed" is all he normally requires.

Thank you, Lord, that I do not have to pray loud or long to be assured of a hearing from you. Nor do I have to work up large quantities of faith to guarantee an answer. You are ready to do more than I ever ask or think. Amen.

TEN. Family Roles ◊

Submit to one another out of reverence for Christ.
EPHESIANS 5:21

L ong before I ever became a psychiatrist, I found myself involved in what is now known as family counseling. Because I was familiar with the biblical script for family role-playing, I would frequently point out to a father, a husband or a wife exactly what the script called for. Very soon I became accustomed to a stock reaction which in summary ran something like this: "Yes, I know the Bible says I ought to love my wife, but it also says she should obey me. And she doesn't. I'll start playing my part when she starts playing hers."

I call this the "Yes—But" Response, and with slight word changes it can be placed in the mouth of any family member. In essence it pleads that one cannot be expected to fulfill one's role in the family properly unless every other member of the family is fulfilling theirs.

I hesitate to dismiss the protest out of hand. Yet you can see at once that it forms an impossible basis for family living. If each family member must first make sure about the satisfactory role-playing of all other family members, or even any of them, the home becomes a forum for endless bickering. Commitment of each member to the unit becomes tentative and fragile. No stability is possible. And the essence of family relationships is that they be—like God's relationship with us—based on unswerving commitment. It is the solid unconditional commitment of family members to one another that makes the growth of rich personal relations possible. (Unfortunately it does not guarantee them.)

This then must form the foundation stone of your relationship to your family. There must be a solid, unswerving commitment to God to play whatever your role may be in the family for his sake and without any regard to how well other family members play theirs. This is part of your Christian commitment. The others may reject you. The family as a whole may turn you out. But until it does, you are committed to God's script for father, son, wife, mother, husband or whatever. Even if the family throws you out, you should be ready at the drop of a hat to resume your role. Each role is played in relation to other roles.

Father, I want to obey you in the family you have given me, even if other family members do not obey you. I know what you have called me to do and be as I relate to others in the family. Give me the patience, love and servant spirit to fulfill that calling. Thank you. Amen.

ELEVEN. You Can Color History! ◊

"It is not for you to know the times or dates the Father has set by his own authority." . . . They all joined together constantly in prayer.
ACTS 1:7, 14

W e are insane. The glories of heaven are ours for the taking. The wisdom of the ages is proffered free. We are bidden to bring our empty hearts to have them filled from cataracts of healing and love. Yet we remain earthbound, fuss-enslaved, parochial-minded and spiritually impoverished. We say we value heavenly things more than earthly, but our behavior contradicts our profession.

Of what value is the life you lead? What will your contribution amount to when the last and final examining board scrutinizes it? Will you have changed the course of history? And if so, for better, or for worse? Is there *any* value in your existence? Or are you destined to be a harmless cork, tossed about lightly on those streams of religious and secular culture that sweep us all from womb to tomb? You were excited by a conference you attended. But for how long? What was its net effect on your usefulness? You were moved by a book you read. What permanent changes did it produce on your character or on the life you will lead ten years from now?

Yet we are invited to collaborate in the creation of destiny, not to be a mere spectator but a coauthor. God does not want to determine all things in splendid solitude by the word of his power. He wants the painting of the future to be a family project in which we all play a part under his benign direction. Earth's policy makers are but actors in a drama written in heaven, and we are offered a pen to do some of the writing. Can we imagine anything better?

I do not say that he intends to reveal to us in a few sessions the whole sweep of human destiny. To do so would pander to our vanity and create the illusion of knowing something that lies beyond our finite grasp. It is not for us to know the times and the seasons. Yet a child who is unable to appreciate the architectural know-how behind the design of a house, or even to read blueprints, may still color the sketches of it or help to build by pounding nails into boards. And both activities (coloring and hammering) are more satisfying to the child than comprehending the technicalities of the plan. Equally important, a good father is delighted to see his child joining in the work.

We are called on to color and to build, not to become pseudoexperts on eschatology.

Creator Lord, you bid me worship you, not understand you. I willingly do so. And I joyfully agree to add my little skills to help with the completion of your splendid plan which overarches all of time and space.

TWELVE. Bad Magic ◊

A tree is recognized by its fruit.
MATTHEW 12:33

There is one source of supernatural power, and one only. Satan's power is power once entrusted to him by God. God was the Creator of the power just as, being the Creator of all that is, he created Satan himself. The power was meant for use in God's service. It is what we might call embezzled power.

And that is exactly what magic is—stolen power, used for the user's delight. Whenever anyone, Christian or non-Christian, angel or demon, uses power for selfish ends (for the love of power or for the justification or glory of the self), the power can be called magical power. It is the same power with the same characteristics put to a wrong use and subtly changed by that use. Christians who use God's power in this way have begun to act like sorcerers. Angels so using it fall.

Because magic is power that was originally created by God, it will always act like divine power in many respects. Its outward characteristics will not distinguish it from godly power. One cannot distinguish divine power from Satanic power by merely comparing certain features of both.

The difference is the difference between dry ice and fire. Both can burn to the touch. But while ice preserves corruption, fire purges corruption and burns away dross. Fire purifies. Fire is clean.

Protect me, Lord, I pray, from all magical powers that would not glorify you by their use. Teach me to discern the difference between your power and stolen power. And bind Satan as he attempts to deceive Christians. Amen.

THIRTEEN. The Value of Faith ◊

Now faith is being sure of what we hope for and certain of what we do not see.

HEBREWS 11:1

F aith is a source of health. Most experienced doctors, whatever their religious views, admit its mysterious influence over the course of disease in some of their patients. Faith also produces emotional calm. Christians in all ages, their lives and faces bearing witness to their claims, have talked of inward peace under trying circumstances. As he ushered them into an epoch of pressure which was to mean imprisonment, terrible opposition and for some of them death, Jesus said to his disciples, "Peace I leave with you" (Jn 14:27).

It was their faith that turned his words into reality.

Faith has enabled reformers to persist against impossible odds to ultimate triumph. It has given courage in battle, hope in despair, and calm in the face of danger and death. It enables us to recognize the power of ideals and truth, even though those who championed them died long ago.

But faith is more than these things. Its highest value lies in its use as a tool by which we may know things otherwise unknowable. Indeed its more immediate benefits spring from this. Faith, by biblical definition, is "the conviction of things not seen" (Heb 11:1 RSV). It is intangible and invisible, serving as a kind of gateway to a realm where other methods of arriving at knowledge will not help us.

But faith comes into its true glory when it operates not within our space-time system but as a doorway leading us beyond it. By faith we can know (curious paradox) that God exists. By faith we can make his acquaintance. Only as we exercise faith will we be able to please him.

Lord Jesus, you call me beyond reason into faith—and beyond the provable things of earth to a kingdom of things not seen. My mind fights against this, sometimes. But my heart knows it makes sense. Thank you. Amen.

FOURTEEN. Peace *with* God ◊

Since we have been justified through faith, we have peace with God through our Lord Jesus Christ. . . . Therefore, there is now no condemnation for those who are in Christ Jesus.

ROMANS 5:1; 8:1

To experience the peace *of* God you must know peace *with* God. And peace with God implies that a state of hostility between God and you is at an end.

Many Christians are deeply confused about their relationship with God. Their theology is divorced from their experience. Their heads can assert truths that their hearts do not appreciate. They know that

Jesus, by his sacrificial death, has paid for their peace with God and that their own faith in Christ secures that peace for them. Yet their consciences haunt them. Specters of sins past and present rise to drive them from the throne of grace so that they stand ashamed and at a distance from God wondering how they may get right with him again. They know, in theory at least, that all their sins are paid for, that God is well pleased with the sacrifice of his Beloved One, satisfied that all accounts have been settled. Yet they feel something is wrong.

They need to feel, personally and in their inmost being, that God is actually forgiving and wiping away all those shameful sins—not the sins of the world, but *their* sins. Then, finally sure of their peace *with* God, they can begin to sense the peace *of* God.

To know such peace is to know that you are loved and accepted. And to know oneself loved and accepted by the living God is to experience a melting away of inner frustrations and angers. I have never known a greater freedom from anger than immediately following my awareness of how greatly I am loved and how freely forgiven.

Thank you, Lord, that nothing can separate me from your love. You are a persistent lover who will always remain faithful to me, even if I am faithless. May I flourish in the greenhouse of your protective, neverfailing care. Amen.

FIFTEEN. Our Country of Birth ◊

And after he became the father of Methuselah, Enoch walked with God 300 years and had other sons and daughters. Altogether, Enoch lived 365 years. Enoch walked with God; then he was no more, because God took him away.

GENESIS 5:22-24

I was born in Britain and lived a good deal of my early life there, but I visited France, Switzerland, the United States, the Caribbean, Egypt, India and Ceylon. However, I never spent long periods elsewhere and always thought of Britain as "home."

I was fascinated by the countries I visited, writing long letters home about them. I even envied many features of those countries—scenery, way of life, climate (Britain's climate is pathetic). But I would not have chosen to live elsewhere. Britain was home.

Later I spent a longer period in the States, married a Canadian there, and proceeded to spend ten years in various Latin American countries. We settled in Canada after that; though I continued to travel extensively, Canada became more like home, and our children did most of their growing up there.

It is now thirty-five years since I left Britain. I have been back for visits from time to time, but with each visit I noticed that Britain was no longer *my* Britain, no longer the Britain I knew as a boy and as a young man. At times the realization was painful. Cities and their streets changed, sometimes radically and totally. Landmarks disappeared. People I knew died or seemed to have grown old when I hadn't expected them to. There was a sort of Rip van Winkle effect after a time, a bewilderment and terrible sense of loss. And of course I had changed too.

The result is that I do not feel totally at home anywhere. You have to be born somewhere to be totally at home there. But you have to spend most of your life there too. I had broken the rule. So now, though I feel more at home in Canada than anywhere else in the world, I don't feel completely at home even there. I talk wrong. I have little bits of Britishness about me that I'll never shed and that will never allow for total assimilation, even in Canada.

But notice the rule. To be completely at home you must be born in a country *and spend most of your life there.* Immigrants may say they are totally at home in the country of their adoption, but I think that in many cases they are kidding themselves a little. It is one thing to be a stranger in the country of your birth, but quite another to be as much at home in your country of adoption as the natives.

A Christian is someone who has been "born from above"—that is, born a citizen of heaven. As Christians read Scripture, the atmosphere of heaven and the culture of the celestial city invades their being. As they meditate, as they pray, as they spend time waiting in silence on God, the same thing begins to happen at an accelerating pace. When they meet and worship with like-minded citizens of heaven, they are really spending time in the country of their new birth. The degree to which they feel at home in the celestial city depends upon the amount of time they spend breathing its air, walking as Enoch did—with God.

I am at home with you, Lord. You are my home. I am at ease, I am secure, I am cared for in you. May I walk with you this day, as Enoch did. Amen.

SIXTEEN. The Great Listener ◊

Come near to God and he will come near to you.
JAMES 4:8

God hears all poured-out agony, but he longs to be something more than a celestial pacifier. He wants people in their suffering to come to him. For he is himself the gift we really need. Children can be placated with candy only for so long. It is the loving parent they want. Therefore go to him in your sorrow.

As Christians we often make two mistakes. We moan fluently to people around us. This may be the lesser evil. Friends can be counted on to take a certain amount of moaning. But we are to bring our griefs to God, and it is here that we fail so lamentably. We come to him. That is to say we exercise faith. We believe he *is*, that he is *there*, so to speak. We also believe that he can hear us. But our fear of God and our reverence for him inhibit us. Can the God of the heavens really care about my little affairs? (Does a mother care about a three-year-old's scratched finger?)

I want to say nothing that will diminish your reverence for God. Some Christians are far too ready to treat God as a heavenly buddy. We are blind to his glory and deaf to the voice that is as the sound of many waters. If I knew how to make you tremble and quake in his presence I would. Indeed I pray that the Holy Spirit may do just that for you.

But to tremble and to be struck dumb need not go together. Great as he is, he is also tender and gentle. And since he is aware of the subtlest nuance of pain in our hearts we need not hide it from him. We may even be angry or resentful toward him, but whether our resentment is justifiable or not, it is better expressed than hidden. Does it shock you, once you see him, to see how horrendous your thoughts really are? Do not disguise them; confess them. Also tell him of your hurts. Time is of no consequence. You may talk for hours since he dwells in eternity where time has no meaning. And know that when you pour out your heart to God, he will be listening intently, understanding profoundly.

Lord, I cannot even talk honestly to you except you help me. Thank you for the assurance that you will listen and understand; help me to get beyond pretending and become wholly honest with you. Amen.

SEVENTEEN. Sin Now, Pay Later ◊

For the wages of sin is death.
ROMANS 6:23

Our calling is a great one. And what we do with our lives is important. We are responsible creatures. Our actions have consequences that matter eternally. When we fulfill our calling, the results are glorious. When we don't, the outcome is equally momentous. The dignity and worth God has given us mean that our successes and our failures both count.

If my son throws a ball through the window, either he pays or I do. Should neither of us shell out cash for a new pane of glass, the whole family pays by suffering the inconvenience of a cold and drafty room. The world cannot remain the same once a ball shatters a pane of glass. You cannot evade the law of consequences.

And nothing in life is free. You may not pay dollars and cents for the air you breathe, but you pay for it by the energy you use to move your diaphragm. Unless you expend that energy, you die. In order to have the energy to expend, you must eat—food that someone has paid for. (Even a mouthful of air can be measured in money!)

The same law operates in the realm of ethics. You can't commit adultery without both paying for it yourself and forcing others to pay too. Even if you and your lover are never caught, you pay in uneasiness, anxiety and a loss of joy in your family.

Moreover, you feel guilty. Guilt means having a sense of the size of the principal that still has to be paid. Your down payment consisted of money, time, anxiety and inner dis-ease. Your guilt feelings are a reminder of that portion of your bill yet needing payment, sometime in the future.

So it goes with any sin, be it pride, anger or dishonesty. Sin is like those commodities you buy on a low-down-payment plan. And the longer you go on, the more the bills pile up (as your conscience quickly will tell you). Thus the plan of "sin now, pay later" has the disagreeable result of pitching you into moral bankruptcy before you know it. And pay later you surely will.

I know what guilt is, Father. Thank you that you do not deal lightly with it; for in my great guilt I have experienced great forgiveness, through Jesus Christ. Amen.

EIGHTEEN. By Design ◊

So if the Son sets you free, you will be free indeed.
JOHN 8:36

Freedom is a lame man walking, leaping and praising God.

Freedom is a woman with chronic obstructive lung disease able to breathe easily.

Picture a woman in a hospital bed. She is overweight and has just finished sneaking a cigarette. She sucks air into herself by an immense effort, neck muscles tightening with each breath. Her lips are blue.

Her eyes stare in fear at the walls of her room. If Jesus were to touch her, or if some miracle injection could give her new lungs, you might (is your imagination vivid enough?) see the fear give place to surprise, then delight. The fight to capture air would be over. Her lips would turn pink. She would get out of the bed and run down the corridor shouting, "I can breathe! I can breathe!" For her that would be freedom.

Freedom is a blind man stepping into light, a deaf girl released from a world of silence, a terrorized victim of political oppression discovering he can express his real opinions to anybody anywhere and can walk out of his front door without checking to see whether the secret police are around.

To be free first means not being what you once were—bound, limited, fearful. Then it means taking a quantum leap closer to what God meant all human beings to be.

Freedom is not "doing what you want." That idea is absurd. We think we know what we want, but we don't. We only know urges and hungers, the pull of illusions. A drug addict "wants" a fix. His "want" is slavery. A murderer "wants" to kill. He is both victim and victimizer. Drug addicts and murderers may be accountable for their actions but, paradoxically, they are far from being free. Do what you like and you will discover you are the slave and the victim of what you hate.

No, freedom is doing what you were designed to do, doing it with power and joy. As a creature formed by God you were designed to serve, love, enjoy and glorify God eternally. In being what you are designed to be you will find joy and freedom.

Lord Jesus, you know exactly where I am not walking in freedom right now. You know how I have tried to redefine freedom according to my own wants—and what has resulted. Forgive me, please. And help me allow you to set me free—by your definition. Amen.

NINETEEN. Where Love Abounds ◊

It is for freedom that Christ has set us free.
GALATIANS 5:1

Y ou can smell social freedom. I remember crossing the Yugoslav border into Austria a few years after World War 2 on the pillion of a motorbike. A friend and I had been contacting a needy church and supplying them with clothing (the bike was large and powerful) and Scripture portions. We had been introduced to both the normal and the underground aspects of the church's activities and had undergone intensive interrogation by the authorities who wanted to track down the destination of the clothing and literature. (They failed.)

We crossed the border into Austria at night. After a few miles I became aware of a sense of exhilaration and joy. To be more precise, I *felt* the exhilaration of freedom, but wondered whether I was just experiencing a psychological release following days of tension. However, I noticed a small difference once the border was crossed. In the Austrian villages through which we passed, people were sitting around lighted tables in open-air cafés.

"Notice anything?" my friend asked.

"Freedom?" I countered.

"So you felt it too. I wondered if it was just me."

It was the little things that cued us to the freedom in Austria. So it is the little things in church life that will cue us to an atmosphere of freedom. Are certain topics taboo? Are certain expressions of concern or affection or joy looked down on? These indicate a lack of freedom. Our actions and attitudes are restricted, inhibited.

Social freedom springs from the loving responsibility of a society's members toward one another. And this in turn springs from their having discovered that God is a God of grace who longs to pardon sinners. The more people perceive the glory of a gracious God, the more willing they are to be open, to repent, to trust him. The more they do so, the more they love one another. And the more people love and care for one another, the fewer laws they need to govern them and the smaller the police force needed to make those laws stick.

If what we are saying is true, then churches where Christian love and responsibility abound (they do not abound in all churches) should be churches where social freedom is both present and felt. Where the Spirit of the Lord is, there is freedom.

Thank you for freedom, Lord. Thank you for the fresh smell of it. Bring it into my church in greater and greater measure, for the glory of your name. Amen.

TWENTY. Long-Range Prayer ◊

Ask and it will be given to you; seek and you will find; knock and the door will be opened to you.

LUKE 11:9

Understanding God's will involves more than intellectual apprehension. My heart has to be prepared, my outlook changed, my values adjusted, my knowledge of God's ways increased. Guidance by God differs radically from any other form of guidance. God invites me to enter into a deeper understanding, and at the same time challenges me about obedience to him. He seeks in these ways to raise me to be a true partner with him.

All this takes time; it cannot be hurried. In my panic I may want instant answers, but instant answers are usually valueless. God spent centuries turning Israel away from idol worship. Likewise, the pains I experience are to be turned to good account. Only as I grow and change am I able to grasp the nature of his will for me and for my children. But I will come away from his presence with more than I ever asked for.

I do not know the nature of your trouble nor the amount of Christian experience you have. But I do know that God desires you to enter into a dialog with him. I cannot tell you how he will communicate with you, but I know both that he wants to and that he is capable of getting through any barrier to communicate his thoughts to you.

Take time. Don't hurry. Spread the matter out before the Lord. Keep a Bible handy as you pray, though not with the idea of receiving guidance like a horoscope reading. Rather it can help you recall godly principles you have forgotten or have been neglecting. Find the passages where the principles are explained. Write down how they specifically apply to your circumstances. As you do you will notice that the tumult in your heart is lessening. Something of God's quietness will bring a measure of peace. Slowly your view of a situation will begin to change, giving place to a new perspective, a changed outlook. You may begin to realize that certain things which seemed crucial are not as important as you thought, whereas others that you had not even considered now seem to be vital.

New objectives and long-range goals for yourself and your children will begin to formulate in your thinking. Commit them to prayer. Be wary of jumping too rapidly to conclusions. It is easy to mistake our own wishes for the will of God. Nevertheless God, who desires greatly that you share in his thoughts, will keep you from straying too far down a mistaken path.

Sometimes I do not understand you, Lord. I pray and you do not seem to answer. But your timing is not my timing. Your wisdom is not my wisdom. I thank you that you do bring my heart into conformity with your heart and so answer persistent prayer. Amen.

TWENTY-ONE. Temporary Residents ◊

The LORD had said to Abram, "Leave your country, your people and your father's household and go to the land I will show you."
GENESIS 12:1

It would be a mistake to call Abraham a nomad. True, he adopted a nomadic lifestyle. But the difference between Abraham and neighboring tribesmen was that, though Abraham had left a settled existence behind, he was looking ahead, as the committed Christian is, to a more permanent one. He was in search of a country where he and his descendants could live in peace.

Abraham never saw his vision turn into reality. Though he found the country he was looking for, he never possessed it. There is a sense in which we possess heaven now, for it is "within us." But in a deeper sense we look for a country that still awaits us. As for Abraham, he remained a wandering stranger in the country he had intended to settle. He is described variously as pilgrim, sojourner and stranger. Were he a child of the twentieth century, we might call him a refugee or a displaced person. Abraham is thus a prototype of the followers of Jesus. We do not live in tents as Abraham the sojourner did. We may not even be called to live out of a suitcase as some of our modern brothers and sisters are. Yet, if we are serious about following Christ, we share Abraham's outlook.

We do not belong. We are temporary residents only. Our real home is not immediately available, but we refuse to settle permanently anywhere else. We are pilgrims and strangers.

We have not chosen impermanence as a preferred lifestyle. We are not nomadic. A nomad thinks only of the next temporary pasture. Deep within us is a longing for our true home. It is this longing that characterizes the people of God. They do not belong to this world— because they belong somewhere else.

Yes, Lord Jesus, I long to be in that eternal home you have promised and prepared. Help me to serve well and patiently here, so that when I arrive I may hear the Father's "Well done." Amen.

TWENTY-TWO. The Power of Forgiveness ◊

The teachers of the law and the Pharisees brought in a woman caught in adultery. They made her stand before the group.

JOHN 8:3

I t was the last thing she had expected.

She had been waiting for death—by stoning. Then, in a way she was at a loss to explain, the accusations ceased to echo from the walls around her. She looked up and discovered the menacing crowd was melting away. At last only One remained.

What now? A cold dismissal? Should she sneak away while she had a chance? Would he say anything? What he did say exploded over her with a power she would never forget.

"Has no one condemned you? . . . Then neither do I condemn you. . . . Go now and leave your life of sin" (Jn 8:11).

No power on earth can touch pardon. Atomic power can vaporize a city. It can raise a mushroom cloud miles into the sky. But it can neither soften a hardened heart, straighten the shoulders of a discouraged person nor break the power of sin.

Forgiveness can do all this—and more.

Father, I have experienced indifference or revenge more often than true forgiveness. Thank you for the times other people have forgiven me, and especially for your amazing forgiveness of all my sinfulness and its outworkings. Amen.

TWENTY-THREE. Peace Can Be Ours ◊

For the LORD takes delight in his people.

PSALM 149:4

Meditation is right when it causes you to worship. If when you contemplate your sin you are able to perceive the wonder of God's kindness in forgiving it and to marvel at the wisdom of a God who forgives it justly, if his divine plan, his incredible long-suffering and patience or the depths of his mercy awaken awe and thanksgiving in you, then you do well to meditate on your sin. Look at it in all its horror and know that the Savior knew of it before he embraced his crucifixion. Contemplate the number of times you have fallen into the same sin and marvel at (but do not presume on) his patience and grace.

The peace *of* God is (among other things) a subjective experience. Peace *with* God is an objective reality providing the basis for the subjective experience. To grasp the nature of your peace with God it is necessary to go back to Scripture and allow the Holy Spirit to flood your mind with an understanding of what Christ has done to establish that peace for you.

Peace means that God and you, you who behave so shabbily to your children or let selfish needs dictate your behavior to those you live with, are reconciled (Rom 5:10). It means that for Christ's sake God accepts you just as you are. It means that he is well pleased with you, indeed that he takes delight in you now that Christ has purchased your redemption. It means that you need have no shame before him but may approach him boldly (Heb 10:21-22). It means that he has, because of the blood of Christ, freely forgiven any of your failures, rages and cruelties that you are willing to acknowledge (Eph 4:32; 1 Jn 2:12).

There is no firmer or broader base for inner peace than to be assured of peace with God. Other roads to peace may secure partial or temporary peace, but only God's peace surpasses human understanding to release us from inner turmoil. The peace exists. It exists for you and is offered to you. Take time to understand it and to find it.

Lord, let me sit with you awhile. Let me see the look on your face as you turn to me. Let your smile banish my un-ease. Amen.

TWENTY-FOUR. Motives for Revival ◊

Revive us, and we will call on your name.
PSALM 80:18

R evival is what we desperately need. And it is God's delight to send it.

First, and above all, we must pray. Indeed we must give ourselves to earnest and persistent prayer. What we term *renewal* is not enough. Dramatic evidences of divine power are of no importance in themselves. If renewal within the church is to fulfill God's purpose for it and if Christ is to be glorified, it must lead to a major evangelistic thrust. It must result in what was once called an awakening in society generally. Only an extraordinary outpouring of God's Spirit will accomplish that.

The awakening must also lead to reforms in society. In the Great Awakening when large numbers were truly born from above, they did more than join churches. By their prayers, their radically changed outlook, their obedience and their example, they changed British society profoundly. A climate emerged in which legislative and political changes followed—the ending of slavery and of child labor, for example—and followed in a way that could and would not ever have been achieved by political activism alone. The changes were a sort of spinoff from the outpouring of divine power.

We must therefore plead for an outpouring of the Holy Spirit on Christian congregations. This seems to be what God would like to give us. We are called to collaborate with him in prayer that it may happen.

And in praying for such an outpouring we must, if we are consistent, pray that the Spirit may be poured out upon each one of us personally. What I ask for the church and for society, I must ask for myself.

My prayers must not, however, be self-seeking. There must be no hidden agenda in my traffic with God. Do I secretly long for an esoteric experience? To seek it will not only be wrong but could be dangerous. Do I long for power and gifts that will elevate me above my fellow Christians? Gifts and power are one thing, but elevation above my fellow Christians is quite another. My desire must be both for God himself and for an empowering that will enable me to serve him.

Lord, teach me to pray aright for revival—first in myself and then beyond. Amen.

TWENTY-FIVE. Prevailing in Prayer ◊

Have faith in God. . . . I tell you the truth, if anyone says to this mountain, 'Go, throw yourself into the sea,' and does not doubt in his heart but believes that what he says will happen, it will be done for him. Therefore I tell you, whatever you ask for in prayer, believe that you have received it, and it will be yours.

MARK 11:22-24

I t is one thing for me to urge persistent prayer for either personal or corporate revival, and quite another for anyone to pray with faithful and unwavering faith. How do you get from being a discouraged intercessor to a warrior who prevails in prayer?

How in particular does one acquire the sort of faith that casts mountains into the sea? To pray for a revival to sweep the land is much more significant, demands a far greater exercise of power than merely tossing Mount Everest into the Indian Ocean. Yet Jesus talks about such feats as though the prayers that occasion them were the heritage of all God's children.

Andrew Murray comments on the key to our difficulty—our difficulty in finding sufficient faith and persistence within ourselves to pray this way. As he examines Mark 11:22-24, he notes that what seem to be Christ's impossibly wild, almost irresponsible claims about the prayer of faith are preceded by the words, "Have faith in God." Faith in God comes before faith in the promise.

Faith in the promise, he tells us, must be an outgrowth of faith in the promiser. You cannot have total, unwavering faith that some*thing* will come to pass unless you have come to know Some*one* well enough to trust him and to know what he wants. Intimacy with a person is involved. The more intimately you know him, the more confidence you have in him, the more clearly you see and hear him. And by the very tone of his voice you know that what he says is true. As Murray puts it, ". . . faith is the ear by which I hear what is promised, the eye by which I see."

God, help me to realize that what matters is not how much faith I have, but how great you are. Amen.

TWENTY-SIX. Guarded Lips ◊

Set a guard over my mouth, O LORD, keep watch over the door of my lips.
PSALM 141:3

Once a young man spread around a piece of criticism (which later proved only half-true) about his elderly pastor which split the church and created a scandal. He later apologized and asked the old man what he could do to atone for his wrong. The pastor grabbed a feather pillow under his arm and took the fellow to the top of the church tower. Wind tugged at their hair, flapping their coattails against their legs as they looked giddily at the village and fields below them. The pastor handed the young man the pillow. "Rip it open," he said.

The boy was perplexed. But he did what he was told. Instantly the wind seized the feathers, tossing them in flurries into the air. A cloud of feathers whirled about their heads, then spread far and wide as thousands of feathers began falling beyond the village, settling on sidewalks, in hedges, in streams, in trees, among deep grass.

"Now," said the pastor, "go and collect all the feathers and put them back in the pillow."

"*All* of them?"

"*All* of them."

"But that's impossible!"

Placing his hand on the young boy's shoulder, the pastor said kindly, "I know. I just wanted you to realize how impossible it is to retrieve a criticism once spoken."

When you are tempted to criticize another person, remember this story. "He who goes about as a talebearer reveals secrets, but he who is trustworthy in spirit keeps a thing hidden" (Prov 11:13 RSV).

Lord, do guard my lips. Help me to resist the urge to criticize and gossip; help me instead to be a trustworthy friend. Amen.

TWENTY-SEVEN. The Glory Unveiled ◊

The appearance of his face changed, and his clothes became as bright as a flash of lightning. . . . Peter and his companions were very sleepy, but when they became fully awake, they saw his glory.

LUKE 9:29, 32

Occasionally God chooses to pull aside the veil which conceals his glory from a man or woman. Christ did so before three of his disciples on the Mount of Transfiguration. Before they saw this spectacular sight, Peter, James and John were living daily in the presence of the Lord of glory. They had learned from him; they had loved him. To be with him had sometimes cheered them and at other times convicted them. But all the while, though they thought they knew him, his glory was veiled from them. Their reactions to it on the mountain were profound. At that point, if I may express it very crudely, he became even more present in their experience than he had ever been before, and they were overwhelmed.

You can get some idea of the effects of such an encounter by thinking of a desert dweller catching his breath the first time he sees the ocean or of a city dweller suddenly placed atop the Matterhorn or of a jaded executive finding himself without warning resting among the silent beauties of coral reefs ten fathoms below the surface.

Yet to encounter God would excite even more wonder, ecstasy, terror or shame than an exposure to his physical creation, however new or dramatic. John fell as if dead at the feet of the glorified Christ (Rev 1:17). Daniel found "no strength . . . left in" him under similar circumstances (Dan 10:8). Isaiah cried "Woe is me! For I am lost" (Is 6:5 RSV). No one who has encountered God in such a way can ever forget what happened. It is a brightly colored page among the black and white of his life.

It is not our job, though, to *seek* such mystical experiences. John was not seeking a vision of his glorified Lord. Isaiah was, as far as we can tell, totally surprised by his encounter in the temple. I know of no one in Scripture who set out to have an experience of this type except Moses, and his encounter had already begun when he begged to see God's glory. God is the one who takes the initiative in communications between himself and his creatures. So if he should choose on occasion to come through on color TV rather than by mail or telephone, that is his business.

I do not know, Lord God, at what moment or for what reason I may need to see your glory in a special way. Perhaps you will show it for no reason of mine. I want to be open to seeing your glory unveiled; to be content with not seeing it. Meanwhile, I will worship you. Amen.

TWENTY-EIGHT. No Other Solution ◊

Did not the Christ have to suffer these things?
LUKE 24:26

The Bible teaches that in the death of Christ is found his triumph over Satan. It also teaches that his death was *necessary*. It was to win something that could be won in no other way. This repels the idea that the Lord was helpless before the Jewish authorities who plotted against him. His enemies were fitting in with his plan. His death was a *must*.

The day Peter blurted out his faith in Christ's divinity, Jesus began to warn the disciples that death lay ahead. Since they knew he was God, he must also make sure they knew his purpose—to die! Peter airily began to take his master to task. Christ's reply startles us by its severity: "Get behind me, Satan! You are a hindrance to me" (Mt 16:23 RSV).

Jesus had to die. He was compelled not by circumstances but because there was no other way to do what he came to do. Any voice that sought to deflect him from his course was to Jesus the voice of Satan himself.

When we ask what made that death so necessary, the Bible does not mince words. He died to *redeem people* and to *forgive sin*. And since, as we have already seen, his death was a must, we conclude that there was no other way in which he could redeem and forgive. If we were to be forgiven and redeemed, *Christ had to die.*

How, Lord God, can the worst event the world has ever seen be the best event? Only because in your sovereign love you allowed this, indeed, designed it as the necessary answer to sin. I do not rejoice that I need Jesus to pay such a frightful price for my sins. But since I do—and there is no other who can pay it—I give you great thanks and praise. In the name of the Crucified One, Amen.

TWENTY-NINE. A Shining Cockroach ◊

Now we see but a poor reflection as in a mirror; then we shall see face to face. Now I know in part; then I shall know fully, even as I am fully known.

1 CORINTHIANS 13:12

Paul Tournier writes about the *persona*, the mask worn by Greek actors to indicate their roles in ancient dramas. He points out that on the stage of life we too wear personas; that is, we assume different personality styles in different situations. We do so by habit. We wear one persona when parenting children, another when asking questions of a lecturer and yet another when being introduced to strangers. In itself there is nothing wrong with this. It makes sense to behave differently when we put our children to bed from the way we do when we give evidence in a court of law.

But there are more sinister reasons for wearing masks. Sometimes we do not want people to see our real faces. We have shames and guilts to hide. If some masks were torn from us, we would be exposed and naked. Our need for acceptance and approval keeps us clutching our false fronts fiercely. Thus we are enslaved to our legalistic facades. It is possible that even those who know us best have never seen all of our faces. We send out antennae like those of a cockroach, probing the atmosphere around us. Our antennae pick up even imaginary vibrations of disapproval and concentrate (have you ever observed a cockroach carefully?) on exterior polishing. Cockroaches actually *shine* in the light. In this respect they are not unlike some Christians who have a surface sheen only.

However unaware we normally are of our personas, we are uncomfortable when we approach God while wearing them. God sees through our masks and we know it. Our souls are naked in his presence. Therefore we shrink from intimate contact with him, hardly knowing why, clinging to our shames and guilts and turning our faces away from him. We resist the freedom we could enjoy if were to let him rid us of our heavy masks.

Lord of truth, help me to discard before you all of the ornate masks I have crafted. Help me to trust that seeing my face you will not despise me but will love and forgive me. Amen.

THIRTY. The Long and Short of Prayer ◊

When I heard these things, I sat down and wept. For some days I mourned and fasted and prayed before the God of heaven.

NEHEMIAH 1:4

P rayer is not something that can be done fast, like speed reading. Some of the great prayers in the Bible were conceived over a long period of time.

Nehemiah, for instance, tells us he prayed for days. Yet the prayer he records can be read aloud in a couple of minutes. Did Nehemiah repeat the prayer again and again for days on end? How do we account for the discrepancy between the length of the prayer and the length of time he tells us he spent in prayer?

There can be no doubt that the days of fasting and prayer were days when God was dealing with Nehemiah. The prayer he records is the end result of many days spent in wrestling with the problem before God. They were days of weeping, of bewilderment, days in which the Spirit of God was laying his finger on Nehemiah's own life. They were days during which Nehemiah's confusion turned to fear as God exposed him to ideas Nehemiah did not wish to entertain. Then came lucidity as he accepted God's will for him. In the end the only specific request he made was that God would protect him from the king's anger.

Like Nehemiah we must go to God with our problems and wait in his presence. We are to express our concerns fully and to tell him of our bewilderment. We are to tell him, too, that we know he hears and that we cannot understand what is happening.

God never mocks people who approach him in this way. He is patient and gentle, and he takes his time. Occasionally he may clarify matters quickly, but more often the process is slow. God has aims in mind besides the well-being of our children. He wants to teach us about himself. The very problems we bring to him serve as the basis of a lesson, a lesson through which we will be changed, our view of him will become larger and the goals we are to seek for our children and ourselves will be made clearer.

Prayer is a great mystery, Father. You want to hear from us and even act on what we say. I don't always understand why you would do this. But you do. And more. You change me as we talk. And I don't understand how this happens either. It is a mystery I praise you for. Amen.

MONTH
FOUR

ONE. True Peace ◊

Peace I leave with you; my peace I give you. I do not give to you as the world gives. Do not let your hearts be troubled and do not be afraid.
JOHN 14:27

A s a medical doctor I have watched many patients being put to sleep under anesthetic. The frowns slip from their faces, and they seem to relax. But they don't have peace; they're just unconscious. I have known people to die, defying God and blaspheming. Afterward their relatives have said, "Ah, now they have peace." But death is not peace either.

Nor do people find peace by calming their nerves or forgetting their worries. You can take tranquilizers to calm your nerves. You can watch television or fall asleep or practice transcendental meditation, and forget worry. But none of these gives peace.

Peace is a deep, heart experience that belongs by right to every Christian. It is a gift Jesus gives us. It is not like the "gifts" we receive from the world. We can choose to rest in it instead of giving place to troubled hearts and to fear.

Was Jesus saying there would be no storms? Far from it. He was about to leave them and was sending them to face problems, opposition, imprisonment and violent death. But in the midst of hatred and persecution they were to have a supernatural gift—the peace of God. It would steady them in the face of threats; it would make them buoyant under a deluge of problems, carefree in poverty and sickness.

The heart that has this kind of peace is like a lighthouse in a storm. Winds shriek, waves crash, lightning flickers around it. But inside, the children play while their parents go about their work. They may look out the window to marvel at the powers that rage around them, but they have peace—the peace of knowing that the strength which protects them is stronger than the strength of the storm.

Lord Jesus, thank you for saying those wonderful words, "Peace I leave with you." Thank you that you say them to me. Help me, please, to look beyond all my anxieties and to claim the true peace you offer. Amen.

TWO. Legalists by Nature ◊

Now the Lord is the Spirit, and where the Spirit of the Lord is, there is freedom.

2 CORINTHIANS 3:17

We are probably all legalists by nature. But certain types of preaching and certain administrators and leaders may worsen our natural tendency. Some church leaders fail to understand the difference between spiritual and worldly authority. Occasionally, especially if they are young in age and inexperienced, they may say, "You must submit to me because God has placed me over you." Now while such words may be true, they are words that never fall from the lips of true leaders because the authority of true leaders springs from spiritual power. Such words prove the speaker's unfitness for his task. They too can enslave us to another gospel rather than draw us to the freedom of the cross.

Legalism alienates us from one another. It creates an atmosphere which inhibits true fellowship. It inhibits our freedom to share our personal weaknesses and ask for help, making some of us suspect we have weaknesses no one else shares or would understand.

We are surrounded by men and women who profess faith in Christ yet are victims of every sort of vice and sin. The sins are practiced mostly in secret. We are also surrounded by a world where these same sins increase daily. Converted sinners are going to need help and deliverance. But from *us*? In the condition *we* are in?

The freedom they need must come from Christ. It will come when hearts (theirs and ours) have been deeply convicted of sin. It will come as we, then they, discover the sufficiency of Christ to shatter the chains of guilt, so that we rediscover overflowing joy and an astonishing reduction of the desire to sin.

Spirit of freedom and grace, help me to leave legalism behind once and for all. Help me to lean only on you to shatter my chains of guilt and to give me joy. Thank you. Amen.

THREE. Where Your Treasure Is ◊

Set your minds on things above, not on earthly things.
COLOSSIANS 3:2

I f we judge by the people who are in modern Israel, we can make a generalization. People from areas of persecution feel the urge to find *home* more keenly than people who are prosperous, settled and comfortable. Thus U. S. Jews may underwrite much of the financing that floats Israel, but U. S. Jews are much less likely to tear up their roots and move there than are Jews who are persecuted in the countries where they live for being Jewish. A New York Jew and a Tel Aviv Jew are two very different people.

There is a parallel in the church. Christians who are prosperous and comfortable on earth may give money generously to Christian work but usually find it hard to think of heaven as home. It is one thing to speak piously about dying as going home, but quite another to deliberately put ourselves in life-threatening danger. Tragically, many who talk piously about "home" display little evidence of longing to be there. Home in Florida is more attractive. Tension exists between home on earth and home in heaven, and there are practical ways in which we can discover where our real interest lies.

Psychoanalysts talk about *cathexis*. Cathexis means (approximately) emotional investment. To cathect something heavily means that your emotional life is pretty tangled up with whatever you cathect. The question that faces every Christian is this: Given that we are less concerned about heaven the more we are wrapped up with earth, and given that the more wrapped up in heaven we are, the less anxious we will be about our earthly home—how much cathexis do we invest in mansions in the skies? I grow weary of the cliché that describes some people as so heavenly minded that they are no earthly good. Years have passed since I met anyone fitting that description. By and large my Christian acquaintances are too earthly minded to be any heavenly good. And this should concern us far more.

Lord, please untangle me from my possessions, my important roles and even my relationships until my cathexis is sufficiently placed in my heavenly home. Amen.

FOUR. The God Who Wants to Answer Prayer ◊

O LORD, God of heaven, the great and awesome God, who keeps his covenant of love with those who love him and obey his commands, let your ear be attentive and your eyes open to hear the prayer your servant is praying.

NEHEMIAH 1:5-6

F aith is not a feeling. It is not even the feeling that something is going to happen in answer to our prayers. Faith may be easier to exercise when such feelings are present. Nevertheless, feelings of that sort never constitute faith. Faith is a response on our part, the obedient response of our wills to who God is and what he says. So notice how Nehemiah's prayer starts: "O Lord, God of heaven, the great and awesome God, who keeps his covenant . . ." (Neh 1:5). His focus reveals the secret of his faith.

You can only have faith in someone to the degree that you know them. In particular you must know two things about them: that they are *able* and that they are *willing* to do what you want them to do. When I was terribly worried about the operation my wife was to have, it was a tremendous relief to know it would be performed by "the Chief." I had seen him skillfully perform the most intricate operations. He never seemed ruffled or upset, however great the crisis. Moreover, he was kind. I knew whom I could trust. He *could* do it, and he *would*. These are the two attributes that Nehemiah saw in God. "The great and awesome God" *can* do everything. The God who "keeps his covenant of love" *will* do anything. Nehemiah doubted neither his power nor his kindness. His God could. And his God would.

I have little problem believing in God's power for I have seen too many evidences of it. But I do sometimes doubt his willingness to act on my account. "Who am I," I constantly ask myself, "that he should take any notice of me?" I am learning about his faithfulness and lovingkindness. My God can. And my God will.

Thank you, Father, that over the centuries believers like Nehemiah have found you powerful and willing to answer prayer. Thank you that you have not changed; you can and will help even me, when I ask. Amen.

FIVE. The Better Man ◊

Do nothing from selfishness or conceit, but in humility count others better than yourselves.
PHILIPPIANS 2:3 RSV

My father-in-law is a Nova Scotian fisherman. He lacks my years of university training. I could talk more impressively than he on world events, philosophy, the limitations of the scientific method and on and on. My vocabulary is vastly greater than his.

But let us put out to sea in a sailing boat off the rocky coast of Cape Breton. He seems by instinct to know the depth of the water everywhere. In an uncanny way he can find any port within two hundred miles in a fog without navigational aids. I become a stupid landlubber, helplessly inept and outclassed by this sea-taught marvel of a man.

Moreover when he visits my home he wanders around noting what needs to be fixed. I am clumsy with tools, bewildered in the face of practical jobs. He fixes my lopsided garden gate. What to me was a formidable difficulty is to him an afternoon's recreation.

Am I a better man than he? By what scale are the two of us to be measured?

Who can say which of us is *morally* superior? I can quote the Bible more helpfully and people are often moved when I preach in public. Through my own prayers and ministry he recently came back to God after years of wandering. Yet now his joy in Christ and in the Scriptures makes me ashamed. He seems to have progressed more in a few months than I in years. With none of the Bible training or helpful influences to which I have been subjected, he has come far. I stand rebuked before him. Who will assess us and tell us which of us is the better man before God?

If I go into the presence of God, the question hangs in the air like an obscenity. I know I have done wrong even to ask it. As the majesty of God fills my vision, all questions of human greatness become pointless. I bend my knees. I fall on my face. I tremble and weep with marvel that such a God calls me his child. I am ashamed of my pettiness, my meannesses, my silly deceits and my ugly greeds—yet simultaneously aware that I am forgiven, wanted, loved. How can I go from God's presence asserting my superiority over my brethren? I count myself happy to be the least of them all.

Forgive me when I compare myself to others, Lord. I don't need to put others down to build myself up because you have lifted me up to the heavens! You have found me of infinite value and sent your very Son to earth to bring me to your throne. How glorious you are! Amen.

SIX. The Father ◊

But while he was still a long way off, his father saw him and was filled with compassion for him; he ran to his son, threw his arms around him and kissed him.

LUKE 15:20

What is the Father like? Jesus described him in Luke 15. He is the father who waits on the rooftop daily for years, straining his eyes at the horizon. (How else would he have spotted the prodigal "while he was still a long way off" if not from a rooftop?)

Yes, the Father is the father who tore out of the house shouting instructions to the servants to prepare a feast, stumbling blindly toward the boy his arms longed to embrace. He is the father who even stifled the son's speech of repentance halfway through as he cried out for a new robe and a ring for the boy's finger. And this Father feels the same way about you and me when we set out to meet him from a distance.

He wants us all to know him as "Abba." When you know him like that your faith will be simpler and clearer, your prayers at once reverent, intimate, informed. You will know what he wants you to ask, and you will want it because he does. You will hear his promises in his very commands, and in the smile with which he lights up your heart.

Did you ever try to call him Daddy? If you're like me you'll find it very difficult. Why? For many reasons. It sounds as though it lacks respect. Yet a child uses the expression without a thought—which is just the point. You see we are talking about becoming little children before the Father. Some of us have grown up saying "Daddy" to our fathers, and as we have grown to maturity (and some of our parents to senility) the word *Daddy* has expressed a slightly patronizing but tolerant endearment—an attitude and posture utterly incompatible with our relationship with the Father of Lights.

He is not "dear old Dad" but the daddy seen through the trusting, adoring eyes of a little child. It is not easy to become a little child. Simplicity comes hard. But if intimacy and power are what we want we must become helpless little children who know him as Daddy.

Abba—Daddy—help me in my awkwardness. I thrill to know the intimacy of being your little child, but it is not comfortable yet in your lap. Help me to feel and trust your embrace. Amen.

SEVEN. Intimacy's Counterfeit ◊

Isn't this the carpenter? Isn't this Mary's son and the brother of James, Joseph, Judas and Simon? Aren't his sisters here with us?
MARK 6:3

S ome of our attempts at intimacy only cause antagonism between us and those we seek to be intimate with, so we have coined the dictum "familiarity breeds contempt." When we attempt intimacy we often go about it in the wrong way. We confuse intimacy with its counterfeit, familiarity. Intimacy is what we want but familiarity is all we achieve. Intimacy is dangerous, a knowing and a being known deeply and profoundly. Casual familiarity may create the illusion of intimacy but it is much safer, having only to do with a pseudoknowing.

The Galileans were familiar with Jesus. They did not know him; they only thought they knew him. They knew his parents. They had watched him grow up as a boy and had observed his developing skills as a carpenter. But their familiarity with him had blinded them to all that he really was. They had nonchalantly categorized him, putting him into the appropriate slot in their minds. Perhaps they had joked casually with him or teased him—their jokes or teasing based on the character they conceived him to have. Their familiarity was a familiarity of what they wanted to see, what they thought they saw.

"Oh yes, I know Jesus," one of them might have said. "Known him since he was a kid. Joseph's son, you know. Good carpenter. Nice kid. Bit quiet at times. Know him? I spoke to him practically every day of his life." They knew him so well, in fact, that he could do no mighty work among them because of their unbelief.

Familiarity is the illusion of knowing in which I see only what I want to see, only that part that I can cope with. Intimacy involves a true knowing.

Lord God, I do not want familiarity with you. I do not want the casual, "Oh, yes, I know the Lord" attitude that is so easy to emulate in order to impress fellow Christians. I want the true intimacy which, astonishingly, you offer to human beings. Help me to find the real thing, I pray. Amen.

EIGHT. Looking Fear in the Eye ◊

The LORD is my light and my salvation—whom shall I fear?
PSALM 27:1

Fear is our enemy. Our victory will begin when we look him in the eye. We must simply face the fact we are afraid. We need not ask ourselves what we are afraid of. Fear feeds on fantasy, and fantasy is an artist skilled in painting unreal horrors. Time spent in viewing them leads to being waltzed through the night in the arms of terror.

We must turn from fantasy to reality. The question, "What do I fear?" must be reworded to, "What is there to fear?" What has changed? "The LORD is my light and my salvation—whom shall I fear? The LORD is the stronghold of my life—of whom shall I be afraid?" (Ps 27:1).

Has my boss's anger changed my relationship with God? Must I equate a broken relationship with divine abandonment? Does a diagnosis of cancer mean that he no longer loves me? Or are the inviolable walls still around me? Could he who said "I will never leave you nor forsake you" break his word? No. His presence will go with us and (if we let him) he will give us peace.

Scripture has a lot to say about fear. "Fear not!" is one of the commonest commands in the Bible. And perhaps the deepest lesson about fear is the one Jesus himself taught. "Do not be afraid of those who kill the body but cannot kill the soul. Rather, be afraid of the One who can destroy both soul and body in hell" (Mt 10:28).

It is true that he was addressing a problem slightly different from the troubles that typically face us. Yet the principle still holds. We fear people to the degree that we fail to fear God. Whatever the word *fear* may mean (respect, reverence, terror) Jesus teaches that we have a choice about the direction in which we turn it and the objects to which we attach it. We may not always be able to quench it, but at least we can then be God-fearing people who use frightening experiences to teach ourselves what the fear of God means and who learn to be free from "the fear of man."

Sometimes my fear doesn't dissolve right away, Lord, even when I realize you are on my side. May my fear of you cause my lesser fears to take flight as I see my problems less and see you more. Amen.

NINE. A Unique Commodity ◊

[Jesus] told them, "This is what is written: The Christ will suffer and rise from the dead on the third day, and repentance and forgiveness of sins will be preached in his name to all nations."

LUKE 24:46-47

C hristianity is the only religion of forgiveness that exists. Muslims pray, fast, give alms and go on pilgrimages. They neither give nor seek pardon. Allah alone is righteous.

Hindus are caught in the wheel of life. Their sins and their goodness are woven into a future existence as a dog or as a worm. There is no pardon—only endless change from one existence to another. Their only hope is somehow to find release from the wheel of life into nothingness.

The religions of early China that formed Confucius's background offer even less. Their loftiest concept of God is of one who watches and judges. There is no forgiveness—only cold, observant disapproval.

But the coming of Christ shifted the focus to a principle deep in God's heart; the idea of "an eye for an eye" was superseded. God was a God who forgave, freely and completely. The past was to be blotted out.

Why I have been blessed with the knowledge of Christian forgiveness, when so many know nothing of it, astonishes me. Accept my thanks and my worship, mighty and forgiving Lord. Amen.

TEN. Two Masters ◊

No one can serve two masters. Either he will hate the one and love the other, or he will be devoted to the one and despise the other. You cannot serve both God and Money.

MATTHEW 6:24

J esus wanted to set us free from mammon in our hearts. "You cannot serve both God and Money," he states categorically. Mammon or money, in the context, seems to refer to care about material necessities. He is concerned, as he always is, with the inner struggle we all experience between things and God.

Quite often we speak of the rat race. Rats may well enjoy (we have no means of knowing) the exercise wheels that accompany their cages. But to humans, the wheel symbolizes the endless struggle of daily living with its depressing sense of never moving forward. It is difficult to avoid getting trapped in a rat race if one lives in the Western world. We are gripped by the delusion that if we earn a little more money, we will be set free. But the carrot of better and finer toys dangles perpetually before our noses, so that we spend more than we earn. To their horror, a couple making $100,000 annually discovers that the goal of freedom is still another $20,000 or $30,000 away. Like a mirage in the desert, the goal has receded from them as they advanced.

Another person may earn $150,000 and feel the bitterness of slavery in his or her soul. You may say, "If I earned that much, I wouldn't feel enslaved," and proceed to tell me how you would go about freeing up your time. But if you are not free now with the income you earn, you will be no more free with fifty times as much. Freedom is an inner contentment with what you have. It means to covet only heavenly treasure.

Thank you, Lord, for the material blessings you have given me. Thank you that you daily meet my needs. Grant me contentment this day in what I have, but mostly, I pray, grant me contentment in you. Amen.

ELEVEN. Grief Work ◊

Jesus . . . was deeply moved in spirit and troubled. "Where have you laid him?" he asked.
   "Come and see, Lord," they replied.
   Jesus wept.
   Then the Jews said, "See how he loved him!"

JOHN 11:33-36

We find it hard to let ourselves feel resentment toward someone who has abandoned us by dying. To resent the dead is too shocking. Yet recognizing not only that anger is normal but also that *anger does not negate love* can bring release. Some bereaved people are unable to mourn, either because they are afraid to discover resentment in themselves or because they consider grief to be a sign of weakness. They should be encouraged to remember times of happiness they enjoyed with the deceased as well as times of conflict. There is no place for locked-away memories following bereavement.

Grieving consists of remembering, of allowing oneself to remember and to sorrow over memories that meant much to us. It consists of coming to terms with reality, the reality that the person who died was human and had weaknesses, yet had endearing traits that were precious and are sorely missed. It consists of realizing, little by little, that one chapter in life is over. It is a chapter that can be reviewed from time to time but that belongs essentially to the past, for a new chapter of life is beginning. We cannot begin a new chapter without having dealt thoroughly with the past.

Some bereaved people feel that they are to blame for the death of someone they love. They may be right or wrong about their belief, but their anxiety and guilt hinder normal, healthy grieving. Usually they experience relief by merely sharing their fear and sense of guilt and discussing it with a sympathetic listener.

A few people will lock up the bedroom of the deceased person. They do not want to face the pain of going through clothing, books and personal possessions that are charged with painful memories. Yet to do so is essential, for "grief work" will not be complete until this is carried out.

I recommend that a close friend or a counselor do this with the bereaved person, usually the day following the funeral.

The symptoms of normal grief (episodic sighing, weeping, a loss of interest in other things) can be expected to last up to two or three months. Some people, because of either heredity or bereavements in early childhood, are high risks for major depressive illness with subsequent bereavements. Such people need more help with their task of grieving.

With wise counsel, our focus and energy will eventually turn toward life. We will leave the dead in God's good hands and get on with the responsibilities—and joys—of the present.

Jesus, you understand my grief because you too have grieved. Help me to grieve as I should—and then to move on. I entrust those I have lost to you, Father. Amen.

TWELVE. The Mystery of Seventy Times Seven ◊

Then Peter came up and said to him, "Lord, how often shall my brother sin against me, and I forgive him? As many as seven times?" Jesus said to him, "I do not say to you seven times, but seventy times seven."

MATTHEW 18:21-22 RSV

L iteralists, numerologists and legalists can do what they like with the calculation. (Some authorities tell us the number is not four hundred ninety times but seventy-seven.) The obvious meaning to the words of Jesus is that there is to be no limit to the number of times we forgive repentant sinners.

The point is also practical. Certain sins, particularly the socially unacceptable ones, are besetting sins. Habits have been formed that are hard to break. Christians who have been alcoholics fall off the wagon from time to time. Homosexuals who have been restored fall back into sinful behavior. Gambling fever which proves easy to throw off in moments of joy, release and forgiveness returns to haunt those who have been gripped by it in the past. We wish it were not that way, but it is. Christ does not give us immunity to temptation, even though we cannot excuse ourselves when we fall back into sin.

After all, are not the most respectable among us subject to our private weaknesses, our angers, our bitternesses, our covetousness? Is it not true that we too have known release from sins and attitudes that return to haunt us in times when our faith seems at a low ebb? Should it surprise us then that our brothers and sisters should experience the same difficulty? Or that they might need to repent and to be received back again and again and again?

Our tendency is to say about someone else's sin, "Once a drunkard, always a drunkard." "She'll never stop her shoplifting. She doesn't really repent. She's just going through the motions to get back in." Hence the seventy times seven. We forgive. We go on forgiving. We never cease to forgive. By all means let us interview repentant sinners, but let us beware of becoming cynics, suspicious, judgmental. For our attitudes will boomerang on our own relationship with God.

In being unwilling to forgive, unable to perceive true repentance in others because the sin has so often been repeated, we open ourselves to the "accuser of the brethren" and begin to lose our own appreciation of God's forgiveness toward us. We become not only cynics, but guilt-ridden cynics. An old Puritan writer once said, "He who fails to forgive, destroys the bridge across which God's forgiveness comes to him."

Most of my sins are respectable ones, Lord. But I know they are hideous in your sight. Please cleanse me through your Son's blood. And help me not to hold back forgiveness from my brother or sister, even when it seems unreasonable to have to forgive yet again. Thank you that your forgiveness goes far, far beyond reason. Amen.

THIRTEEN. Bought Back from Bondage ◊

For [I came] . . . to give [my] life as a ransom for many.
MARK 10:45

———————————————————————————————

J esus himself said so. He did not only say he came "to seek and to save" people. (You can interpret those words several ways.) He came to *redeem* them. He came "to give his life as a ransom for many" (Mk 10:45).

But is not that saying the same thing? Not necessarily. Some say that Jesus *saves* us by his death, but they do not think he redeems us. He is Savior. He is not, according to them, redeemer. He saves us, they say, by the beauty of his example. When we realize how great God's love is, it so affects us that we undergo a change. That change constitutes our salvation. Christ's death was necessary as a moving example of God's love. It operates psychologically.

Now Christ's death does indeed touch our hearts. But it does much more. To ransom, in New Testament times, meant to pay a price in order to release or buy back something (or someone) in bondage. In our case we were "in bondage" because of our sin. Sin had put us under a sentence. We were drowning in moral debt. And the Son of man came to give his life to ransom us from that situation. The ransom price he paid was his own life.

Again I hear this truth, Lord Jesus. And again I am astonished. You thought I was worth all that? Then, since you ransomed me, I am your willing slave. Use my life as you will. Amen.

FOURTEEN. Calloused to Awe ◊

Go into the rocks, hide in the ground from dread of the LORD and the splendor of his majesty!
ISAIAH 2:10

W e must watch out for the tendency to be too casual, even to be flippant, in modern approaches to prayer. God used to be a Benign Granddad. Now he is becoming a Celestial Chum. We may be striving for honesty, openness, a break from ritual and stereotype, all of which are good. Conversational prayer, for instance, can be a breakthrough for some people. But because we are human, we are calloused to awe.

Recently I conducted a prayer meeting for some Christian leaders. After Scripture reading and some sharing I suggested, "Let's spend time together in worship and adoration so that our requests will come into perspective as we remind ourselves of the majesty of God." They all nodded eagerly, but it was clear from their prayers that no one had understood.

"Thank you, Lord, for the privilege we have in approaching you," ran one prayer. "Thank you for your many blessings. Please help us, O Lord, to be obedient to you. Bless the services in the church and grant that . . ." Or someone else would pray, "Thank you, Lord, for reminding us that we ought to worship you more. Forgive us for our failure to do this. Forgive us also for not being more loving to one another. Help us to be more faithful day by day, witnessing by our lips as well as by our lives. Bless the many missionaries. . . ."

Thanksgiving, yes. Praise for practical things, even for spiritual blessings. But with a sinking heart I realized that those who prayed were blind to the majesty and glory of God.

I could not be critical of such prayers. But it was obvious to me that had the Christian leaders been granted a vision of a glorified Lord, the content of their prayers would have been more God-centered. Their prayers might have been, "Lord, as we see you as you are, we marvel that you are interested in us at all. We are overwhelmed by your glory. We can only say, 'Worthy are you, O Lord, to receive honor, praise dominion and power.' We fall on our faces before you and are delighted to know that we are creatures of your creating, slaves by you redeemed. Your love is incomparable and we have no words to magnify it enough."

May the Holy Spirit remind us that we need to learn to tremble, as well as to be close.

Lord, I do marvel; I am overwhelmed. Praise be to you. Amen.

FIFTEEN. The Three Faces of Worldliness ◊

Do not love the world or anything in the world. If anyone loves the world, the love of the Father is not in him.

1 JOHN 2:15

Do not love the world." To what world does the apostle John refer? To the age we live in with its values and goals. What then are the things in the world that we are to eschew? "For all that is in the world, the lust of the flesh and the lust of the eyes and the pride of life, is not of the Father but is of the world" (1 Jn 2:16 RSV).

Is the apostle oversimplifying things? Can our age be summarized so succinctly? Indeed it can. Worldliness is not a list of do's and don'ts. Its essence lies in three lusts—of the flesh, of the eye and of pride. It is an attitude of heart. *To be worldly is to have one's heart-love stolen away from the Father and replaced by lusts.*

There is the lust of the flesh, by which John may refer to legitimate bodily appetites (for food, sleep, sex and so on). These become lusts when we raise them to the level of demigods before whom we bow and for whom we live. In that case lusts are legitimate appetites to which we have become slaves. Or else John could be using "flesh" in the Pauline sense of the term, referring to carnal lusts, the worship not merely of normal bodily appetites but of sinful appetites as well.

The lust of the eye is the worship of beautiful things, the desire and the will to possess them. There is nothing wrong with beauty. There is nothing wrong with wanting something beautiful. The question is: How much is it wanted? More than we want the Father's will? What price are we prepared to pay to get what we want?

As for the pride of life, the pride against which all of us struggle, it requires no explanation. It needs only conviction and repentance.

Can worldliness be reduced to three simple principles? John seems to think so. Let us adopt another expression for lust—*the pursuit of pleasure:* the pursuit of bodily pleasure, the pursuit of possessions that give us pleasure and the pursuit of excessive self-esteem and respect of others that give us pleasure. To pursue these things is to be what is known as a hedonist. And what we are saying is that Christians and Christian churches have been desensitized to sin by hedonism.

Let us be very clear about the matter. There is nothing wrong with pleasure. All the devil can do is teach us how to abuse it. But we are bombarded by the values that control the world around us. We have been brainwashed into believing that certain things are *necessary*, that we deserve more, that we have our rights (including the right to have every physical and emotional need satisfied right now). In our worldliness we have adopted the perspective of the age we live in.

There are more important things than sex and self-esteem here and now. For we are at war with principalities and powers. And from time to time war calls for sacrifice, pain, suffering and bone weariness.

Lord, thank you that you know about unmet needs. Thank you that something more is offered to me than worldly gratification which never really satisfies. Help me to focus my heart-love on you and you alone. Amen.

SIXTEEN. The God of Compassion ◊

As a father has compassion on his children, so the LORD has compassion on those who fear him; for he knows how we are formed, he remembers that we are dust.

PSALM 103:13-14

G od is not only merciful, he is compassionate and understanding. He knows. He remembers. He is aware of our feelings, our weaknesses, our inadequacies, and knowing them he enters into our experience and sympathizes. He is under no obligation to do so save for an obligation to his own nature. He would not be true to himself were he not to enter into our experience with compassionate understanding. In this capacity he is also acting as a parent. We may count on that understanding for it is always present.

But upon our shoulders rests an equal burden. Because we are understood, we must understand. Because we are pitied, we must pity. The measure of compassion we receive must be the measure of compassion we give.

There are times when our ability to give runs totally dry. We pour ourselves out for others and still they need more. We seem to see no change. We become too hurt to care for anything but our own pain. "How many more times?" we ask in despair, feeling that our store of compassion has long since been exhausted. Yet we have a Father whose compassions never fail but are renewed morning by morning. To him we ourselves must turn and drink compassion until our thirst is quenched, allowing his inexhaustible fountains, his endlessly gushing springs of compassion to wash over and through us. As Mary Shekleton writes,

> I am an empty vessel—not one thought
> Or look of love I ever to Thee brought;
> Yet I may come, and come again to Thee
> With this, the empty sinner's only plea—
>   Thou lovest me.

We must think about the compassion he has toward us, thanking and praising him for it whether we feel it or not. For it is real. It flows over us even when we least perceive it. In thanking him our own dry wells fill again.

Oh, you who are the wellspring of compassion, spring up in me till my whole body is saturated. Then let me see the world around me through changed eyes. Amen.

SEVENTEEN. It Is Written ◊

Have you never read . . . ?
LUKE 6:3
It is written. . . .
LUKE 4:4
The Scripture cannot be broken.
JOHN 10:35

J esus often told people, "It is written . . ." and then challenged them to obey the teachings recorded in Scripture. Those who have done so, through the centuries, have found their lives changed.

An atheist once publicly challenged Harry Ironside of Chicago to a debate on their respective beliefs. Dr. Ironside accepted the challenge but proposed that his opponent bring to the meeting a hundred persons whose lives had been revolutionized for the better by atheism. The atheist could not. Dr. Ironside then stipulated that ten people only were necessary. For himself, he promised to bring ten Christians whose lives had been delivered from drunkenness, lying and pride by the Word of God. In the end the poor atheist had to confess that he could not produce even one person and gave up the debate. No more eloquent testimony to the claims of Scripture could be found than the lives of those who read it.

How can we convince others of our position? There is no need to do so. While we should always be ready to explain why we believe that the Bible is the Word of God, divinely inspired, there is little point in laboring to convince our friends of this. They must find out for themselves.

Charles Spurgeon, the well-known preacher, said that to defend the Bible is like defending a caged lion. It is foolish, he pointed out, to stand outside the cage with a drawn sword to protect the lion from its attackers. The most effective way to defend the lion would be to open the cage and release it. The Bible, like the lion, is well able to look after itself. The best way to convince people that it is the Word of God is to encourage them to read it for themselves with an open mind.

The same applies, of course, to us. I have not written this to remove your doubts about whether the Bible is truly the Word of God. If you want to be convinced of the truth of what I am saying, do not study what I have written. Take down your Bible and read it. Read it prayerfully. Read it carefully. And, above all, read it with a willingness to put it into practice.

You will find that instead of your mastering it, it will master you. Such is the power of the Word of the living God.

Lord Jesus, help me to obey the written Word so that my life may please you who are the living Word. Amen.

EIGHTEEN. Avoiding Needless Suffering ◊

They picked up stones to stone him, but Jesus hid himself, slipping away from the temple grounds.
JOHN 8:59

J esus created a sensation by raising Lazarus from the dead. The tide of his popularity was running strong. Everyone clamored to see him. And that very popularity constituted a threat to the authority of the religious leaders. In an emergency meeting of the Sanhedrin, Caiaphas the High Priest made it plain that Jesus must die. His suggestion quickly turned into serious planning (Jn 11:45-50). Jesus was aware of the danger—and deliberately sought temporary obscurity in Ephraim on the edge of the desert.

On another occasion there is a hint that something miraculous took place when the crowd tried to lay hands on him. The mob wanted to lynch him and mysteriously Jesus "walked right through the crowd and went on his way" (Lk 4:30).

If Jesus was resolute in facing death on some occasions, he was equally quick to avoid it on others. Why? Was he stronger on some days than others?

The New Testament never suggests that sacrifice and suffering are in themselves good. Jesus faced the cross because it was the only way sinners could be redeemed. He "endured the cross, scorning its shame" (Heb 12:2), not because it was virtuous to do so but because suffering and death were the price he had to pay to achieve his purpose.

This is important. Religious teachers down the ages have taught ascetic techniques, sometimes because making yourself suffer heaps up merit points for you but more often as a kind of Spartan training by which you subdue your rebellious body to a point where you can be truly spiritual. Such suffering is found nowhere in the life of Jesus. Although he was poor, there is no suggestion of asceticism in his lifestyle. Indeed he was accused of being "a glutton and a drunkard" (Mt 11:19) simply because, as he himself acknowledged, he ate and drank like any other person of that day. If he fasted or spent time in prayer, he had a purpose in doing so. He was not training himself to subdue his bodily appetites. When finally he faced his passion, it was because "the hour" had come. Jesus was not a masochist, a Spartan, or an ascetic.

Jesus' attitude will serve as a model for me as I face suffering too. He faced redemptive suffering with fierce resolve, seeing as Satanic anything that would turn him aside. But he saw no virtue in suffering for suffering's sake, and he avoided it where possible. Moreover, his outlook on suffering was not morbid, neurotic or masochistic. He saw beyond the pain to glory and victory. And it was the prospect of glory to the Father, of salvation for humanity and of victory over darkness that impelled him to overcome the shrinking of his flesh and to march forward resolutely, trampling death under his feet.

We are invited to walk in the steps of a conqueror.

I do not seek suffering for its own sake, Lord. But if it should come as a result of obedience to you, give me the courage and strength to face it well for your sake. Amen.

NINETEEN. Take Up Your Cross ◊

Unless a kernel of wheat falls to the ground and dies, it remains only a single seed. But if it dies, it produces many seeds.
JOHN 12:24

I cannot stress strongly enough that *there is no virtue in suffering itself.* It makes no sense to choose to suffer when you don't have to. You prove nothing by lying across a railroad track and letting the train amputate one of your legs. But if, in rescuing a child from an oncoming train, you lose a leg, then the amputation, disastrous as it may be, constitutes a badge of sacrificial courage and a reminder of the value of human life. Such suffering has merit.

When Jesus tells you to take up your cross daily, he is not telling you to find some way to suffer daily. He is simply forewarning of what happens to the person committed to following him. The phrase has no mystical significance. It is neither a call to seek suffering as an end in itself nor an invitation to undergo an inner experience of dying. "If you want to follow me," he is saying, "be prepared for what you will have to face. They put me on a cross—and they may do the same to you. They ridiculed me—they will ridicule you. You will do well, then, to arm yourself daily with a willingness to take whatever may come to you because of me."

If we face the cost of following Jesus realistically, and if we face it every day, we will in fact face a deeper kind of dying, a "kernel of wheat" kind of dying. We will die to the lives we once wanted to live. We will die to our right to control what happens to us, to our ambitions, our right to choose, indeed to every "right" we think we have.

We must therefore look at both aspects of commitment to Jesus—the risk of unpleasant things happening, and the deeper question of the death that must precede the experience of resurrection life here and now.

From childhood I have been taught that I have certain rights. Help me to relinquish these, Father, so that your kingdom may be spread broadly by my life. Amen.

TWENTY. Why Quiet Time? ◊

Happy are those [whose] delight is in the law of the LORD, and on his law they meditate day and night. They are like trees planted by streams of water, which yield their fruit in its season, and their leaves do not wither.

PSALM 1:1-3 NRSV

Regular sessions of prayer and Bible study produce changes—changes in us and changes in people around us.

Our values alter once we start meeting regularly with God. Some things that once seemed important shrivel and lose their fascination, while others swell in significance. Seeing life through different eyes, we begin to adopt a heavenly perspective, growing more akin in our thinking to the celestial than to the earthly host. Inevitably we will influence people wherever we go because we carry with us the smell of heaven. We will nauseate some and awaken in others a longing for Christ.

We will see people differently. We will pity people we once feared; eschew people we once cultivated; pray for people who once enraged us. The changes do not result because we mechanically follow rules, but because we have our new way of seeing, a new way of savoring life on earth.

We will, to be sure, approach problems differently, feel different about our work, our studies, our job, our future. Our goals will have changed so that life slowly takes on new meaning. The changes are understandable since we are influenced by the people we associate with. The more powerful or the more distinctive the characters of people we rub shoulders with, and the more time we spend with them, the greater the likelihood of change. It follows that if we spend time daily in the company of our Creator God, a profound impact will be made on our existence.

The changes need not be permanent. A tree that bends in the wind can straighten when the wind stops blowing. Leaves that turn from the shade will turn again when the shade is removed. But let the wind blow from the same quarter year in and year out to affect the tree's growth and development, and we shall observe a permanent molding in its shape. Or let the sun for years shine splendidly from above and we shall see great boughs spread symmetrically to rise sunward and retain their form come darkness, earthquake, gale and blizzard.

So it is with time spent with God. A Christian, like a tree, never ceases to grow. As godly influences are incorporated, so changes which at first were temporary themselves become settled parts of our character that resist change. To have a quiet time regularly will produce permanent and beneficial changes.

Lord, I want to see life through your eyes. I want to be shaped by the wind of your truth. I want the smell of heaven to be on me. Thank you for allowing me to rub shoulders with you, mighty and loving God! Amen.

TWENTY-ONE. Listening for God ◊

I will stand at my watch and station myself on the ramparts; I will look to see what [the LORD] will say to me.
HABAKKUK 2:1

P rayer must never be a monolog. True prayer is always initiated by God and represents our response to what God is saying.

We may not always realize that God is speaking. If we are aware as we begin to pray that whatever drives us to prayer is in fact God's way of drawing us into his presence, we shall approach him with greater confidence.

Everyone who prays knows that praying is more than asking and receiving. I begin to ask and I sense that something is wrong. The Spirit of God turns the course of the conversation. I want to talk to him about Mrs. Green. He wants to talk to me about my sin. I want to talk to him about Africa. He wants to talk to me about my next-door neighbor. I come armed with a list of subjects for prayer. He comes to me with one thing that he wants me to do. It is only in my hours of quiet waiting on him that he is able to sort out the confusion in my mind, showing me how he really wants me to pray.

For God's promise is his extended hand. And when we reach out we are startled to find we have touched life and power. We have grasped the mountain-moving hand.

Indeed we shall discover that in praying we have merely been responding to the Holy Spirit's prompting. We supposed the prayer was ours, only to discover that it was orchestrated by him. Our advocacy has been part of a mysterious pas de deux. We have prayed ourselves into a joyful surprise.

Precious Lord, I thrill at the realization that you invite me into conversation with yourself. I want to learn to hear your voice, not merely to exercise my own, in prayer. Help me properly to approach you; help me properly to respond to you. Amen.

TWENTY-TWO. Ordinary People ◊

I praise you, Father, Lord of heaven and earth, because you have . . . revealed [these things] to little children.
MATTHEW 11:25

We know who Jude meant when he spoke of "the faith that was once for all entrusted to *the saints*" (Jude 3). They did not wear halos, nor were they distinguished from their brethren by any special sanctity. They were the ones who had been called to salvation. They were the ordinary Christians who made up the church. Among them were many ignorant and unlettered men and women. It is surprising and humbling that the great and unfathomable revelation should have been made to such simple souls. The Lord Jesus on one occasion actually thanked the Father that he had revealed eternal truth to "babes" or "little children."

This is a forgotten lesson. We are too quick to be influenced by the teaching of people who by their own confession are not Christians in the New Testament sense. We should, of course, respect learning and we must never be obscurantists. But it is significant that Jude should point out, as did his Master, that the revelation was given to *saints*, not to universities, not to the best thinkers of the day.

We need be neither surprised nor alarmed if these (the best universities and the best thinkers) do not agree with God's revelation. Great as their wisdom is, they are capable only of producing something that will change with time.

To us has been given a divine revelation. It is the one thing certain in the midst of change, the sure Word which stands as a rock above the shifting sands of changing thought. Let us pay heed to it. Let us contend for it ardently.

It is wonderful, Lord, that you accept—and even use—both the sophisticated and the simple. Thank you for calling me to salvation, thereby making me a "saint." Thank you that halos are not required. Help me to cling to and defend the sure Word. Amen.

TWENTY-THREE. Waiting on the Lord ◊

The eyes of the LORD are on those who fear him, on those whose hope is in his unfailing love, to deliver them from death and keep them alive in famine. We wait in hope for the LORD; he is our help and our shield.

PSALM 33:18-20

Often I read the third chapter of the book of Lamentations to pathologically depressed patients. Hope is something that is almost always possible. The crux of Lamentations 3 is the poet's refusal to relinquish hope in God.

The only connotation of hope in modern preaching seems to be eschatological. Yet hope is precisely what distressed people need. It is the forward-looking equivalent of faith, faith in what God will do eventually because of who he is and because his mercies are daily renewed. I therefore take my seriously depressed patients to biblical passages written by profoundly depressed people (it is always a comfort to know that "people in the Bible" were sometimes cast down) and insist that as long as God is true to his name, hope is possible.

The best attitude of seriously depressed people is to quit struggling for instant happiness and to hope and quietly wait for the Lord. By this I do not mean that they must be passive or that they must avoid medical or psychological intervention, but their progress will be faster and their anxiety greatly relieved if they can grasp that hoping and waiting quietly for God's time are vital to the battle.

The Scriptures have much to say about "waiting upon the Lord." Many different Hebrew words are translated by the English word *hope*. Some have the connotation of silence or stillness (Ps 62:1, 5; 65:1). Others imply an active choice to await a response (Job 32:4, Ps 33:20; 16:13; Is 8:17). One word, *yachal*, means specifically to wait expectantly or to wait with hope. Indeed the word is translated "hope" more frequently than "wait" (Job 14:14 and Ps 33:20 as "wait" and Ps 33:18 as "hope"). Translations seem to differ as to whether *yachal* should be translated "hope" or "wait" in different contexts (Job 6:11 RSV and KJV).

Waiting hopefully, expectantly and with quiet endurance forms a theme in both the Old Testament and the New. Indeed a good preparation for anyone engaged in counseling would be to do word studies on Greek and Hebrew words translated "hope" and "wait" in English. We have forgotten the importance of such an idea in our age of instant, ready-made solutions. Because I have never heard a sermon on hope, I presume that our preaching may reflect our cultural bent toward instant solutions.

Lord God, enable me to look past my worries and fears and to actively hope in you. Give me peace in waiting, even when I cannot yet see what I am hoping for. Thank you. Amen.

TWENTY-FOUR. The Indwelling Spirit ◊

And with that he breathed on them and said, "Receive the Holy Spirit."
JOHN 20:22

I t is difficult to conceptualize the Holy Spirit's relationship with us as believers. Our bodies have a certain volume. We are temporal and dimensional beings who, because we have not experienced eternity, have difficulty understanding what eternity is.

God, on the other hand, inhabits eternity. He is spirit. In one sense he does not occupy any space—that is to say he does not, like us, have a specific volume that can be measured. In another sense, of course, he fills all space. If you are a Christian, the nonspatial Holy Spirit indwells you, may even fill you. Since he is a person we could say that all of him is inside your body. (You can't have only part of a person inside your body.) Yet I and every other Christian have all of him too. In him we all become one, yet without losing our individual identities. But such ideas can be confusing if we think of an infinite person being "crammed into" each one of our little bodies. We conceive of ourselves as separate from one another, largely because we occupy separate chunks of space.

Since we automatically think in spatial and temporal terms, we must be careful as we look at the terms the Bible uses in describing the Spirit's operations in and upon us. Indeed the two little words *in* and *on* generally relate to two distinct aspects of what the Holy Spirit does for God's people. He is *in* all of us all the time. He comes *on* us for specific purposes at certain times. When he comes on us he is sometimes said to fill us. And though it may seem confusing to us that he could come on or upon someone he already lives inside, the confusion has to do with our inability to think in anything but spatial terms. Prepositions are helpful, and the Scripture uses them, but we must try to use the terms just as the Scripture does, without letting spatial concepts confuse us too much.

And if some remains a mystery to us, we can still rejoice that God has chosen to dwell in such a frail form as ourselves.

I am amazed that you live not only with me but in me, Lord. I find great joy in having such intimacy with you. Thank you. Amen.

TWENTY-FIVE. Truly Converted? ◊

All those who heard [Saul] were astonished and asked, "Isn't he the man who raised havoc in Jerusalem among those who call on this name? And hasn't he come here to take them as prisoners to the chief priests?" Yet Saul grew more and more powerful and baffled the Jews living in Damascus by proving that Jesus is the Christ.

ACTS 9:21-22

I n the early days of the revolution in China, many Christians were shaken by the uncanny similarities between communist and Christian indoctrination. Mass youth rallies rang with joyful singing. When the atmosphere was "right," testimonies from communist converts radiated the joy and purpose their new faith had brought them. Dynamic preachers swept audiences along with torrents of irresistible Mao-speak. Sacrifice was called for. Appeals were made. Specially trained counselors dealt with interested inquirers. And Chinese men and women went through an experience which seemed weirdly to ape Christian conversion, at least outwardly.

More recently, many Christians have experienced déjà vu as they have seen hundreds of cults populating the countryside. And they have been jolted by what they have seen. Unfortunately, the phenomenon of conversion was for them the great rock on which their faith rested. Having seen hundreds of people turn to God in response to gospel preaching, they *knew,* or thought they knew, that the gospel was true; yet if a Moonie or a Krishna or any cult member was converted to his or her cult in the same way, by the same methods and with the same psychological results (joy, peace, new zeal) as someone who was converted to Christ, what could this mean?

It means simply that conversion is a psychological phenomenon. People or events can be behind it as easily as the Holy Spirit.

The truth of Christianity, however, does not rest on the fact that Christians have been converted to it. We are sure that Jesus is God and Savior because God raised him from the dead. So our faith rests on a historical fact, not on a psychological phenomenon.

Further, while *some* Christian "conversions" have a merely human origin, not all do. The genuine Christian conversion is accompanied by something that God does within a person. It is accompanied by spiritual as well as psychological changes, and by a progressive change of character as well as by a redirection of enthusiasms.

In spiritual conversion the emotional changes are the results of God's working, for he gives rise to all the fruits of righteousness. In a purely psychological conversion they result from a technique or from emotional pressure. True Christian conversions are not the result of proper evangelizing techniques. They are a miracle of grace.

Holy Spirit, thank you for your transforming work in my heart, based on Christ's work on the cross. Lord Jesus Christ, thank you for dying so that I can live—eternally. May my life ring true to others who need true conversion. Amen.

TWENTY-SIX. Justice Comes Down ◊

For the LORD is righteous, he loves justice, upright men will see his face.
PSALM 11:7

Our Father in heaven is just. His response to our sin is appropriate. It is never excessive and never reflects his petulance. Moreover, he has always gone to the trouble of finding out exactly what the situation was in which we sinned. He relies neither on angelic gossip nor on demonic tattling.

"I have indeed seen the misery of my people in Egypt. I have heard them crying out because of their slave drivers, and I am concerned about their suffering" (Ex 3:7). God had seen, had heard and knew for himself. Again, before he inflicts doom on Sodom we hear him say, "I will go down and see if what they have done is as bad as the outcry which has reached me. If not, I will know" (Gen 18:21). God's omniscience is not a passive status quo but is active.

He has always been just with you when he has afflicted you. He has considered every angle, taken every factor into account. As he is to you, so he demands that you be with others. He deplores impulsive outbursts based on inadequate information. Rather he demands that you inquire carefully and thoroughly and wherever possible (for he understands that you cannot be omniscient as he) that you satisfy every avenue of inquiry when action may be required.

Again his concern for justice is such that he never backs away from unpleasant issues, and he demands that we not back away either. It may at times seem judicious to turn a blind eye to wrongdoing, but we must never do so either because we ourselves fall short of God's standards or because we lack the courage to face the resentment of others. He calls us to be faithful to his just standards.

Thank you, O God, that your justice toward me has all my life been the justice of mercy. I have not so behaved with the people around me. Teach me to be to them as you have always been to me. Amen.

TWENTY-SEVEN. The Value of Confession ◊

Therefore confess your sins to each other and pray for each other so that you may be healed.

JAMES 5:16

R oman Catholics often think of confession as something you go to—at least once a year, say, at Christmas or Easter. Protestants prefer not to think about it at all. Isn't there something unhealthy about focusing on personal sin, especially in public? ". . . whatever is pure, whatever is lovely, whatever is admirable . . ." (Phil 4:8). Not scandal! If we are given the privilege of going to God's very throne, and in secret, should not this be enough? "No," James stubbornly insists, "confess your sins to *each other*."

It is sometimes easier to confess a sin to God than to one's neighbor. Yet confessing a sin to a friend can give me the kind of relief that confessing to God does not. My friend is "real," and so my confession to my friend represents a real transaction.

God is real too. Yet we sometimes wall him off and he ceases to be real to us. We treat him with unconscious contempt. It would bother us to shock or grieve a friend. But God's grief and shock no longer affect us. We do not feel them. We say we reverence him and we believe what we say, but we do not even respect him. We would experience more relief from getting matters straightened out with an angry garbage collector than with an angry God. Our understanding of God's grace has become devalued to what Bonhoeffer derides as "cheap grace."

Here then is the rule: If it fills you with deep shame to confess to a close friend what is easily confessed to God, then your confession to God is in some sense unreal. The shame validates the transaction. Confession is not merely a verbal description of thoughts and actions. People who truly confess to God no longer care whether others learn their secret. The relief that floods them is such that it flushes away their shame as well as their guilt.

The practice of confessing our faults to another human being can in fact make the Godward transaction more real. Confession is meant (among other things) to heal.

James's exhortation ends with the words, " . . . and pray for each other so that you may be healed." Physical and emotional disease can arise from unresolved sin. Confession is meant to involve a real encounter with a real person. It is intended to produce healing. If the encounter with a fellow human can help the divine encounter become more real to us, then we had better take a serious look at the practice of confession.

Help me, God, not to underestimate sin nor undervalue grace. Enable me to bring to you—directly or with the help of another person—everything which needs your cleansing touch. Enable me to be open to my friend's prayer for me, and to your healing of my soul. Amen.

TWENTY-EIGHT. Honesty in Witness ◊

Let your light shine.
MATTHEW 5:16

To let my light shine demands *honesty*. It demands honesty before unbelievers. Witness is not putting on a Christian front so as to convince prospective customers. Witness is being honest, that is, being true to what God has made me, both in my speech and in my day-by-day behavior.

Such honesty will demand that we talk about Christ to unbelievers with whom we converse. The fact that we have in the past had to create openings to talk about spiritual things proves that subconsciously we have been avoiding the openings that are continually being presented to us.

We all hide our real selves behind a front. To preserve the image that we create, we must talk, laugh, behave in a certain way. Our talk is designed to create an impression on people we talk to, build up or preserve the image of ourselves we wish to sell. Now, for many of us, *witnessing* means adding certain Christian features to this image. But in doing so we are preaching ourselves, not Christ.

Real witness, on the other hand, means abolishing the front behind which we hide, not modifying it. To live behind a front is to hide our light. It is falseness; and falseness is opaque to divine light.

Now if we are even partially honest (total honesty is rare and difficult) in a conversation with an unbeliever, we will find it extremely difficult to avoid talking about Christian things. Do you say it is difficult to witness? I maintain that, with a little honesty, it is almost impossible *not* to witness.

Lord, I am adept at leaving the work of witness to someone with stronger conversational skills. Help me, please, not to cheat those around me who need to hear of you. Help me to be honest as I speak about what you have done for me. May people be helped, and may you be pleased. Amen.

TWENTY-NINE. Living Beyond Time and Space ◊

For thus says the high and lofty One who inhabits eternity, whose name is Holy: I dwell in the high and holy place, and also with those who are contrite and humble in spirit, to revive the spirit of the humble, and to revive the heart of the contrite.

ISAIAH 57:15 RSV

W e lead limited lives, if size is anything to go by. We live on the head of a pin for five minutes. Lost in vast reaches of space and time, lost by very reason of our smallness and our circumscription, our lives resemble popping flashbulbs seen from ten miles away.

Consider for a moment how you are trapped in time. We journey at a rate we have no control over. We cannot return to the past, our own or anyone else's, except in memory or imagination. Nor can we hurry ahead to see how the land lies and make provision for it. Controlled by powers we do not understand, we are driven by another in the prison-coach of time.

We are limited too in our contact with ideas and truth. The most widely read person among us has only rubbed shoulders with a few obscurity-bound professors or dipped into a selection of "the world's great books"—a contradictory jumble of finite perspectives. Yet we are invited to private tutorials with the fountain of ultimate wisdom; to a daily audience with the author of history; to fellowship and communion with the source of all holiness and love.

There is no charge for such privileges. Yet strangely, we pour out our substance to purchase vastly inferior ones, scrabbling among straws and garbage while a jeweled crown is offered to us.

To commune with God is to touch both infinity and eternity, not metaphorically but in very deed. We have opened a window to both a beyondness and an immediacy which time and space are powerless to provide and which we can experience in no other way. To that degree we have broken away from time-space to discover infinity close at hand. No astronaut can slip from beneath "the bonds of earth" more truly than he or she who touches God. Do you want to escape the confinement of a bodily existence? Meet God in your quiet time. He dwells in eternity and his being is infinite.

O mighty and infinite Lord God, thank you for your offer to take me beyond the confines of time and space. Thank you for your wanting to teach me, for wanting to spend time with me. Forgive me for often being too busy for you. Help me draw close to you. Amen.

THIRTY. The Lamb Who Is the Lion ◊

I did not hide my face from mocking and spitting. . . . Therefore have I set my face like flint. . . .
ISAIAH 50:6-7
As the time approached for him to be taken up to heaven, Jesus resolutely set out for Jerusalem.
LUKE 9:51

I t is sentimental to view the crucified Jesus as a lovely model of passive anguish. In truth he is an active conqueror, grappling powerfully with sin and death. He is our champion, scorning his own life that he might batter down the prison doors and set captives free.

He Hell, in Hell laid low.
Made sin, He sin o'erthrew,
Bowed to the grave, destroyed it so
And death, by dying, slew.
Bless, bless the Conqueror slain!
Slain in His victory!
Who lived, Who died, Who lives again
For thee, His Church for thee!

There is nothing morbid about the sacrifice of Jesus. The music of the Passion must be written in a major, not a minor, key. He looked on the travail of his soul and was well pleased. He saw beyond his death to the army of the redeemed, drawn to him in salvation when he was lifted up.

And though he sweated great drops of blood, though he knew spiritual and physical agony, his death was the death of a strong man binding the god of this world. We speak of him as the Lamb of God to remind ourselves of his purity, not of his passivity. We do well to remember that he is also the Lion of the tribe of Judah.

I praise you, Lord Jesus, for you chose to endure humiliation and you triumphed in it. I thank you that you did that for me. Amen.

MONTH
FIVE

ONE. The Leap ◊

The LORD will guide you always.
ISAIAH 58:11

I remember climbing up a cliff from a beach when I was young. I had no experience in climbing, but the cliff lured my hands and feet with tempting holds and breathtaking possibilities. My object was to reach the highway on the mountainside above the beach. Unknowingly, however, I had selected a point where the road cut through a tunnel beneath a huge shoulder of mountain that jutted into the sea. As I climbed my fear and perplexity grew. Surely I should have climbed far enough to reach the road by now! Yet endlessly the steep mountain face rose above me.

It was only when I decided to climb down that I perceived with horror how far away the beach was. The descent looked infinitely more difficult than the climb. I knew I would never make it down. Then I saw the road emerging from the mountain over on my left. But how to get there? I froze. I knew I could reach up with my left hand to grab a ledge of rock above me and so proceed to the left. But my muscles refused to respond. Trembling and sweating I clung to the face of the rock.

A trivial detail assumed absurd significance. From beneath the ledge above me a bunch of nettles projected. I would have to put my left hand through them to seize the ledge. They would sting me. Foolishly I tried to work out ways of extricating myself without touching the nettles.

I don't remember how long I hung there. I knew that I was being absurd, that nettle stings were a trivial matter compared with life. Yet only with an incredible exercise of will was I able to overcome my obsession and plunge my arm through the nettles and seize the ledge. From that point it was plain sailing.

Our fears about the will of God make us freeze in the same way. We cling to our precarious footholds rather than risk the unknown. It is one thing to believe in the intellectual proposition of a loving, omnipotent God. It is quite another to entrust our destinies to him. We grow anxious and fearful as we become aware of how much hangs in the balance. We close our minds to what God would say, understanding only what we have already experienced.

Sometimes I am paralyzed by indecision, Lord. I think and weigh and consider and talk and when it all comes down to it, I am afraid to choose. Free me from this lack of faith and give me the confidence to trust you as I make decisions. Amen.

TWO. Peace and God's Word ◊

Great peace have they who love your law, and nothing can make them stumble.

PSALM 119:165

An eminent psychiatrist once told a friend of mine that he recommended solid Bible study to all his neurotic patients. He was not a Christian, yet he had discovered the peace-giving effects of the Bible.

The psalmist says that people who love God's law will have peace; "and nothing can make them stumble." In modern English the last part of the verse would read, "and nothing shall upset them."

Mind you, I am not saying that the Bible is a tranquilizer. Peace comes when the truth of the Bible throws light on our heart's problems. It becomes even deeper when we put what the Bible says into practice. "If only you had paid attention to my commands," cried God on one occasion, "your peace would have been like a river" (Is 48:18).

Is there something God has spoken to you about from his Word? Does he want you to do something but you are putting him off? Could this be the way you lost your peace? Well, it is not worth it. Give in to the Lord and do it. You will be amazed at the peace that will quietly fill your soul.

Lord, I want to be a calm river, not a raging torrent. Help me to pay attention to your commands—and to find peace. Help me to reflect your peace to those around me, as well. Amen.

THREE. Three Kinds of Giving ◊

They gave as much as they were able, and even beyond their ability. . . . but they gave themselves first to the Lord and then to us.
2 CORINTHIANS 8:3, 5

We need to become willing to give of ourselves to one another. And this in turn is related to the genuineness of our giving of our time and our energy to God. Yet Christ's emphasis seems more on the matter of giving money. Why? Is there some relationship between the two, between the willingness to give of ourselves (our time and emotional energy) and our willingness to give our money away?

Indeed there is. True generosity in one area commonly coincides with generosity in the other. Christian communities where there is generous self-giving are usually those characterized by financial generosity. Both are connected with giving our very persons to God. And while many of us feel we have already given ourselves to God, it may be that we have done so with many unconscious reservations.

Consider how the Macedonian churches gave to the Jerusalem relief fund. Paul describes it at length to the Corinthians: "And now, brothers, we want you to know about the grace that God has given the Macedonian churches. Out of the most severe trial, their overflowing joy and their extreme poverty welled up in rich generosity. For I testify that they gave as much as they were able, and even beyond their ability. Entirely on their own, they urgently pleaded with us for the privilege of sharing in this service to the saints. And they did not do as we expected, but they gave themselves first to the Lord and then to us in keeping with God's will" (2 Cor 8:1-5).

There we have it. Financial generosity, giving oneself to God and giving oneself to others—all mentioned in the same passage. It is not the order in which the three occur that matters. Ideally it should follow the order Paul gives. In real life it may not. But the three belong together.

Lord Jesus, on days when I feel I have nothing to give—no energy, no time, no funds—work in my heart as you did in the Macedonians. Bring me to the place where I can feel it a privilege to give "in a wealth of liberality" even beyond my comfort zone. Amen.

FOUR. Uniquely Crafted ◊

All you have made will praise you, O LORD; your saints will extol you.
PSALM 145:10

Mia gave us a teapot.

Mia is a woman who has a knack of winning the confidence of teenage kids in trouble. She is also observant and thoughtful. Two things about the teapot struck me. First, it was beautiful—unglazed, dull red, exquisite in shape and overlaid with ceramic flowers. The other thing I noticed was that she had spotted an empty niche near our fireplace that was waiting for something like that teapot. Her choice was a hand-and-glove fit. Mia proudly told us, "It's unique. The craftsman made only one like this."

A week later the Changs came over for coffee and Dr. Chang spotted the teapot. "Why I do believe . . ." he began as he crossed the room toward it. "Yes, it *is*. These used to be made in a village near where I was born. The earth there . . . it's different from anywhere else." There was growing excitement in his voice. "I remember exactly how they made them." He paused and his wife leaned over and spotted Chinese characters on the inner surface. "They're very rare," he said. "Even in China. . . ."

Craftsmanship. It has little place in our technology-dominated world. I have three handsome plastic plant pots, all identical and from the same mold. I bought them because I liked them. What care I if five thousand others were manufactured? Mine are still beautiful. The curse of technology does not lie in its capacity to multiply beauty but in its ruthless suppression of creativity. It is not what it does to things that matters, but what it does to people. The workers who pulled my plant pots off the assembly line probably felt nothing at all as they did so. But the person who made the teapot must have been proud and satisfied.

Thank you, Creator God, that though I feel very ordinary at times I am your unique creation—you made only one like this. Please complete in me those good purposes which you had in mind from the beginning. Amen.

FIVE. Buried Longings ◊

A longing fulfilled is a tree of life.
PROVERBS 13:12

We were visiting Macau, the Portuguese colony on the Chinese coast. We had set out early so it was still morning when Pastor Lam, a former Hong Kong football star and a power for the gospel in Macau, took us to the church James Morrison built years ago. We visited his grave and the graves of his wife and their children, many of whom died very young.

I stood silently at the foot of Morrison's grave and began to sob. I did not understand why I was sobbing. I had never met Morrison; indeed, he died long before I was born. I had not even thought about him for years. I wept episodically all that day. I had only to think about Morrison's grave and I would start to cry again. I tried to talk about it once or twice, but I had to give up because I would wind up weeping. What was happening to me?

It was only later that I understood. I had read about James Morrison many years before, moved by the role he had played in the evangelization of China, by his translations and by the Chinese dictionary he produced. His role had been highly significant in the earliest days of Protestantism in China. But what was it that so moved me?

The Portuguese have a word for it—*saudade*. It has to do with the deepest longings of your heart. And my longing was to be where the battle was, where Jesus was, and to experience the reality of God himself. In some mysterious fashion the solidness and reality of Morrison's grave had brought me into contact with the greater reality I longed for. As I touched the gravestone and read its inscription, God reached through and released intense longings so deep within me that I had not realized they were even there.

I have news for you. You have those same longings. Buried, perhaps, and hidden from your consciousness, but waiting to be awakened. It's Augustine all over again. There is a tug, a hunger buried in our hearts, an unease that will never be satisfied until God's purposes for us are fulfilled. It will stay there until our hearts find rest in the God who placed it there. The finding may be sudden or gradual, perhaps more likely in a series of clamberings and crises, until we are altogether committed to him.

Lord, may my longings be for you and for your will in my life. May I not give up my search to fill that hole in my heart till it is filled with you. Amen.

SIX. Prayer and Feelings ◊

If, when we were God's enemies, we were reconciled to him through the death of his Son, how much more, having been reconciled, shall we be saved through his life!

ROMANS 5:10

Sometimes we confuse faith with *feelings of faith*. The two are not the same. When we lack appropriate feelings (like the feeling that God is near or that prayer is a delight and relief) we tend to lose heart. Our prayers seem to bounce back mockingly from the four walls.

God does not require feelings of faith nor should we strive to produce them. He does want faith, but faith is not a feeling so much as an attitude of our wills. By faith I defy my inner states and say, "I cannot feel you, Lord, but I know you are present and I know you can and will hear me." To pray like that is to begin to exercise faith. I should not look inside for appropriate feelings but at the invisible, unfelt God, and address my words to him by a defiant act of faith.

Reluctance to pray this way may arise from a vague sense of guilt, an inarticulate feeling that our prayers (as distinct from those of better Christians) will not be heard because they don't deserve to be. If so, our feelings deceive us. By all means we should confess the sins we know about and wish to abandon, and by all means we should be open to the Holy Spirit's conviction of specific sins. But if, as is so often the case, our prayers are hampered by an unfocused sense of uncleanness or unworthiness, then we are being fooled.

You and I have been made worthy. We have been adopted into God's family. Having acknowledged our sinfulness and having looked to Christ for redemption, we are complete in him. To be sure, our struggles against sin have often wound up in defeat. Nevertheless, provided we do not attempt to cover up or to pretend we are better than we actually are, our moral imperfections are taken care of by our Redeemer.

If feelings of guilt arise (which may represent nothing more than mortification), we should ignore them. We must lay aside false shame and praise the Savior who made us worthy to enter the holiest place of all. We must do as the writer to the Hebrews urges us (Heb 4:16): "Let us then approach the throne of grace with confidence, so that we may receive mercy and find grace to help us in our time of need."

Oh, Father, it's hard to pray when I don't feel like it. I may feel tired or guilty or angry. Thank you that I can express the feelings to you without fear of condemnation. In fact, when I come to you I can receive your mercy and grace. Amen.

SEVEN.   God Is a Consuming Fire ◊

Then [Moses] said to them, "This is what the LORD, the God of Israel,
says: 'Each man strap a sword to his side. Go back and forth through
the camp from one end to the other, each killing his brother and friend
and neighbor.' "

EXODUS 32:27

We feel sickened by the atrocity of sword-carrying Levites slashing their way through cowering ranks of guilty Israelites and killing three thousand of them in an orgy of retribution (Ex 32:27-28). But to Moses the bloodshed was not to be compared with the horror of the people's sin.

"Turn from your fierce anger," Moses beseeches God, "relent and do not bring disaster on your people" (Ex 32:12). Bold words indeed. It is the boldness of a bear at bay with her whelps, of a lioness whose kittens are threatened. Moses is oblivious to personal danger. One thing matters to him: that Israel be delivered from the consuming fire. This is the Moses we must see when we think about the slaughter in the camp.

Have you ever prayed like that? Have I? Are we in fact supposed to? Clearly we cannot work ourselves up artificially to the pitch of feeling that impelled Moses along his perilous course. Yet why is it that we go our ways unconcerned by the judgments of God that threaten his people today, smiling our evangelical smiles and praying, "God bless our church, Amen"?

Is it that we have never visited Sinai? Never seen the burning holiness of the God whose laws express the consuming fire of his being? Have we become so drenched with the spirit of the age we live in that sin has become a theological technicality? Does the prospect of divine wrath and judgment strike us as remote? Inconceivable? Do we, worse still, see pleading for God's mercy as being incompatible with the once-for-all sacrifice of the Lamb of God?

If you are to know the boldness and passion of Moses' prayer you must stand where Moses stood. You must see our God as a consuming fire. You must stand in his presence and listen to the uncompromising clarity of his judgments and laws. Read again the books of Exodus and Leviticus. Read them prayerfully and with an open heart. They are, though you may have forgotten it, still part of Holy Writ. Do not be afraid to let their standards grip you. Kneel down in awe before the pillar of fire. Your vision has been distorted. Your values are corrupt. Only as you let his Word sink deep into your will, will you see sin for the horror that it is. Only then will you know that no step is too drastic to deal with it. Calvary makes sense only in the light of Sinai.

Holy God, in light of your righteous wrath I can only plead, undeserving, for your mercy. I, my family, my church, my nation do not deserve your goodness. Thank you for the death that brings life. Amen.

EIGHT. God's Initiative in Prayer ◊

The word of the LORD came to Abram in a vision.
GENESIS 15:1

U nlike many of us, Abraham had no problem making contact with heaven. He never needed to try. Throughout his long life it was God who made contact with Abraham.

We are not always told exactly how God did so. Often we read, "The Lord said to Abraham . . ." with no explanation whether God spoke in an audible voice or in the stillness of Abraham's heart. One time God spoke in a vision (Gen 15:1); on another occasion he "appeared" to Abraham (Gen 17:1). The important point to grasp is that each time communion between the two is mentioned, God took the initiative. God spoke and Abraham responded. Our prayer lives will be much simpler if the same proves true for us.

And why should it not be so? We think of praying as talking, and certainly talking is involved. But the quality of a conversation may well be determined by the person who initiates it. Indeed our whole reaction to a conversation often depends on who first started it. It is comforting, in a group of strangers, to have somebody greet us and show a friendly interest. It may on the other hand be difficult for us to start a conversation, and it becomes doubly so when our attempt is met with a cold stare.

God is always speaking. To hear his voice is not usually a mystical experience. It consists merely of a willingness to pay heed to the God who lays a claim on our lives. It is, as Hallesby once pointed out, "to let Jesus come into our hearts." For the word *hear* in the New Testament does not commonly refer to an auditory experience. More often it means "to pay heed." "There's none so deaf," we used to say in the north of England, "as them as *won't* hear."

Abraham, then, was not unique. God approaches all of us in the same way. To hear him involves no exercise in "tuning in to the right frequency" so much as a humble recognition that it is his prerogative to speak and our responsibility to respond.

Lord God, I am taught to work hard at the Christian disciplines. Yet you bid me simply listen and respond. Help me in my confusion. And teach me to properly let you into my heart and life. Amen.

NINE. Unpleasantness ◊

Remember the words I spoke to you: "No servant is greater than his master." If they persecuted me, they will persecute you also. They will treat you this way because of my name.

JOHN 15:20-21

We may need to take the risk of unpleasantness. In the Gospels Jesus points this out a number of times. "I am sending you out like sheep among wolves," he told the disciples. "Therefore be as shrewd as snakes and as innocent as doves. . . . All men will hate you because of me. . . . A student is not above his teacher, nor a servant above his master. . . . If the head of the house has been called Beelzebub, how much more the members of his household" (Mt 10:16-25).

In other words, whenever you do something Jesus may send you to do, you will get the treatment Jesus got—sometimes acceptance, sometimes rejection. You will be treated as he was treated. Some people will be drawn to you as bees to honey. Others will hate the ground you stand on.

If you are open and honest—true to yourself and true to Christ—your life will provoke hostility in some and will powerfully attract others. To some it will be "a savor of life unto life" and to others "of death unto death." If you are faithful to him, it may make you unpopular and unprosperous. Of course, it may have the opposite effect too.

The question is: Do you, in fact, put Christ first, *whatever* the relative cost?

Jesus, help me to be open and honest about what you mean to me. I know I don't need to be an international evangelist. All I need is to be free to acknowledge the facts of my life—that you are my Lord and that I follow you. Grant me this freedom, I pray. Amen.

TEN. Looking at the Blackboard ◊

You will keep in perfect peace him whose mind is steadfast, because he trusts in you.
ISAIAH 26:3

We need to get into the habit of *fixing our eyes by faith on the Lord.* The psalmist spoke of the person whose "heart is steadfast, trusting in the Lord" (Ps 112:7). That's what we might call the steadfast gaze of faith. And Scripture guarantees it will result in peace. "You will keep in perfect peace him whose mind is steadfast," says Isaiah, "because he trusts in you" (Is 26:3). So don't look at problems. Look at the Lord—fixedly.

This is important. If we have fears or anxieties that rob us of peace, the Holy Spirit will give us peace by making real to us the power and love of God. But we've got to cooperate. He can't make God's love and power real if we persist in fixing our minds on our problems.

A teacher can only make the lesson plain to the pupils who are looking at the blackboard. The Holy Spirit is a teacher. Let us fix our gaze therefore on the One about whom he wants to teach us.

Lord, I become distracted and my eyes wander, I get weary and my eyelids droop, I look at myself with fascination and see nothing else. Please forgive me and help me learn to focus my eyes and my mind on you. Then, keep me in the perfect peace which is your promise. Thank you. Amen.

ELEVEN. Rejoice ◊

Rejoice in the Lord always. I will say it again: Rejoice!
PHILIPPIANS 4:4

Let me state the obvious. Place your hope in something unstable and you can count on nothing. Circumstances are unpredictable. Future reactions of friends or family under stress cannot be foreseen with certainty. Hope built on anything so ephemeral as our subjective impression of current progress is a structure built on sand.

Faith rests ultimately not even on what God will do but on who God is. We may be mistaken about his future purposes and even more mistaken about what the future holds. But we need never be mistaken about who he *is*. He is faithful. He is compassionate. He is just. He is accessible.

There is sound logic then in Paul's injunction, "Rejoice in the Lord always." It is the first signpost on the road to parental peace. And if the road to which the signpost points should seem impossibly steep, take heart. It is far from impossible. Your first steps will be slow, and you may need to pause for breath from time to time. But by and by your legs will grow sturdy and your chest more expansile.

Since you cannot rejoice in the future, you must learn to rejoice in the Lord. Be clear what Paul is saying. He does not exhort us to be happy, but to rejoice, which is quite different. Happiness may come or go. In a sense you have little control over it. There is no verb "to happy." Happiness is not something you can *do.* Joy on the other hand is. We can and should *rejoice.* That is to say, we can and should say with the prophet Habakkuk, "Though the fig tree does not bud and there are no grapes on the vines . . . yet I will rejoice in the LORD, I will be joyful in God my Savior" (Hab 3:17-18).

Whatever the exhortation to rejoice may seem to be, it is not a shallow cliché but a call to life and health. It is a call to detach our tendril hopes from crumbling walls in order to train them to climb solid rock.

You are the solid rock on which I stand, Lord. When I build the foundations of my hopes and dreams on you, nothing can shatter them. While everything around me may change, you do not. So I rejoice in you. Amen.

TWELVE. Setting Our Affections on Things Above ◊

The mind controlled by the Spirit is life and peace.
ROMANS 8:6

S ome years ago on a seven-hour flight I settled down to pray. But, try as I might, I couldn't. I felt ill at ease and had no peace. I knew what the trouble was. It seemed likely that we'd have to move to another mission field where costs were high. After four years in Bolivia we had built an adobe house and had scraped together some bits and pieces of furniture. We could only sell at a loss. How could we manage in Argentina? Oh, I knew the Lord wouldn't let us starve, but I was unhappy.

Quietly I thought of a verse of Scripture, "I will never fail you nor forsake you." But it didn't work! It gave me no peace. Determined that it should, I opened my Bible and hunted it up. This is what I read: "Keep your lives free from the love of money and be content with what you have, because God has said, 'Never will I leave you; never will I forsake you' " (Heb 13:5). I knew what was wrong at once. I was bothered about security on earth when I should have been thinking of treasure in heaven. I confessed my sin and my peace was restored.

Are you haunted by unrest? When carolers sing about "peace on earth," does it seem to you a mockery? Well, God is offering you a special gift. He paid a tremendous price for it, but he wants you to have it.

Give more time to his Word. Stop resisting God when he speaks to you through it. Ask him to teach you more about the blood of his Son. Stay your heart upon Jehovah. Stop fretting about earthly security. Seek treasure in heaven.

As you do so, you'll find a great, perfect, inconceivable, unearthly peace that will flow on and on like a river.

Prince of peace, accept my praise that you are peace and give peace. Help me claim what you offer; help me set my affections not on earthly security but on the things above. Amen.

THIRTEEN. Avoidable Suffering ◊

When you are persecuted in one place, flee to another.
MATTHEW 10:23

We must not be gluttons for punishment. Jesus does not urge his followers passively to accept any persecution that comes their way. In the context in which it is found, "Take up your cross" means something similar to "Take your life in your hands." It means: "Be prepared to carry your own noose around with you, to run the risk of anything, even death itself. Don't seek death. Avoid it if you can, and get the gospel message to anyone who will listen. If men threaten you, go someplace else where they will listen."

During the fifteenth and sixteenth centuries, the Roman Catholic Church rightly opposed a doctrine of some mystics that become known as quietism. Quietists taught that since God is sovereign, everything that comes to us comes directly from God. And quietists went on to say that we should therefore resist nothing we encounter in life, but receive whatever comes quietly and without any resistance. We must receive everything from God as part of his training for us. To resist suffering is to resist God.

The quietists went too far. I may certainly trust God about everything I encounter. Certainly he accepts the responsibility for the fact that it has touched my life. And certainly I must thank him for the fact that even in that circumstance he will be faithful to me and bring good out of it. But he does not expect me to be passive in the face of evil.

When he tells me not to resist evil but to return good for evil, he is not telling me to take no steps to deal with my headache—and surely not to let thugs beat an old lady to death. It is true that Jesus tells us to return evil with good, but sometimes the good must take the form of removing the temptation to do evil out of a violent person's way.

Lord, I need to be able to discern what comes from your hand and what does not. Grant me this wisdom so that I may work against what is evil and cooperate with your good. Amen.

FOURTEEN. Peace Restored by Love ◊

For he himself is our peace.
EPHESIANS 2:14

The most frequently quoted words from John's Gospel do not read, "For God so hated sin, that he gave his only Son, that whoever believes in him might be made righteous." Such a statement would be true. But God is even more concerned about sinners than about sin. He loved "the world" of sinners. He is the shepherd desperate over one lost sheep, the woman searching for her lost silver coin, and the father wildly delirious over the return of his erring boy (Lk 15:1-32).

The gospel is the story of a loving God reaching out to people. Paul, as God's servant, tells us he preaches the gospel because love forces him to (2 Cor 5:14). Love, he tells us, reconciles us to God (2 Cor 5:18). Indeed if God reconciled us to himself while we were shaking our fists at him, how much more, having been reconciled, will he treat us with mercy now? (Rom 5:9-11).

Such love makes our salvation more than ransom from merited punishment. Something has happened to us. We have been given hearts that instinctively cry, "Abba"—"my very own dear father!" (Rom 8:15; Gal 4:6). God tells us, "I will be a Father to you, and you will be my sons and daughters" (2 Cor 6:18). We receive "the full rights of sons" (Gal 4:5). Such is God's mercy. And so great is the love he bears us that he has "raised us up with Christ and seated us with him in the heavenly realms in Christ Jesus, in order that in the coming ages he might show the incomparable riches of his grace, expressed in his kindness to us in Christ Jesus" (Eph 2:6-7).

Once "far away," we "have been brought near through the blood of Christ. *For he himself is our peace*" (Eph 2:13-14). Christ preached peace to us, his enemies, so that instead of being estranged from him we might become members of his very household (Eph 2:17-19).

Need we quote more Scripture to demonstrate that reconciliation is what the gospel is all about? That justification and redemption were but the costly means by which our restoration to peace with God was secured?

Father, what wonderful promises your Word gives. It guarantees that you have provided for me reconciliation and a future too fantastic to yet grasp. In awe I thank you for all that, and for what it cost you. Amen.

FIFTEEN. Clinging to God ◊

Jacob was left alone, and a man wrestled with him till daybreak.
GENESIS 32:24

J acob wrestled with God because he had no choice. He was defending himself, not attacking. Yet the end of the narrative states that he had won a victory. "Your name will no longer be Jacob," he was told, "but Israel, because you have struggled with God and with men and have overcome" (Gen 32:28). The name *Israel* means "God strove." So far so good. We can rest assured that if God strove, then God was indeed the initiator of the struggle.

In what sense then did Jacob overcome? Read the narrative again. Picture the wrestling as God seeking to help Jacob understand something. Picture him as urging upon Jacob truths that Jacob is unwilling to see. Picture him, as they struggle, trying to convince Jacob that he means no harm, that his intentions are not malicious but merciful. (Often I have had to seize delirious patients as they rush terrified into the Canadian snow. I am the aggressor, yet my purpose is merciful.)

But Jacob is too afraid. All his life he has learned one lesson: It is safe to trust no one. Jacob must fight his own battles. So he wrestles on, terrified by unyielding. Then, suddenly—incredible pain and a useless leg.

Have you ever tried wrestling with lumbago or a slipped disc? If you should ever find yourself in Jacob's situation, let me tell you what you will do. You will cling. You will hang onto your opponent with desperation. Either you cling or you fall.

And through the fog of pain and terror the words begin to penetrate Jacob's brain: "Let me go, for the day is breaking."

Let him go? How can he? He isn't even sure whether he can walk. Let him go? How dare he? At some point the awful knowledge has gripped him that the one on whose breast he leans sweating and gasping is the God of his fathers, who could slay him with a glance. And for once, since he has no choice, no other hope, Jacob's tenacity is turned in the right direction.

"I will not let you go, unless you bless me."

They are words God has waited over forty years to hear. He would have preferred that Jacob recognize his helplessness and cast himself on the mercy of his God long before. He did not wish to reduce him to such an extremity, but Jacob had left him little choice. Now God's response is swift in coming. Jacob has conquered by his helpless dependency.

For me as well, mighty God, it is hard to learn my own helplessness. I want to cast myself on your mercy now, before you have to wrestle me to the ground. Teach me a healthy dependency, Lord. Then meet me in my helplessness. In Jesus' name, Amen.

SIXTEEN. Becoming Like Us ◊

At that time Jesus came from Nazareth in Galilee and was baptized by John in the Jordan.
MARK 1:9

As a medical student I once missed a practical class on venereal disease. Because of this I had to go to the venereal diseases clinic alone one night at a time when students did not usually attend. As I entered the building, a male nurse I did not know met me. A line of men were waiting for treatment. "I want to see the doctor," I said.

"That's what everybody wants. Stand in the line," he replied.

"But you don't understand. I'm a medical student," I protested.

"Makes no difference. You got it the same way everybody else did. Stand in the line," the male nurse repeated.

In the end I managed to explain to him why I was there, but I can still feel the sense of shame that made me balk at standing in line with men who had VD.

Yet Jesus shunned shame as he waited in line with sinners to be baptized. He refused to gather his clean robes around him or to emphasize how different he was. And the moral gulf that separated him from us was far greater than that separating me from the men at the clinic. Moreover, my dislike of venereal disease was as nothing compared with Jesus' utter abhorrence of sin.

But he crossed the gulf, joined our ranks, embraced us and still remained pure. He identified with those he came to save. He became like us.

Lord Jesus, thank you that you counted the shame less important than the sinners who were shaming you. Thank you for joining our ranks. And thank you for bringing to wretched human beings your glorious salvation. Amen.

SEVENTEEN. Oil on Troubled Waters ◊

Let the peace of Christ rule in your hearts, since as members of one body you were called to peace.
COLOSSIANS 3:15

We speak of "pouring oil on troubled waters." The metaphor springs from the curious way oil makes tumultuous waves subside by changing the surface tension of water and reducing the effects of wind. Rescue operations from wrecked ships have occasionally been made easier and safer by pouring oil on the sea surrounding them.

To become a source of peace is to become oil on troubled waters.

Becoming oil is not a technique by which you psych your family into tranquility. To do so is to play the diplomat, the very thing we need to supersede. To be oil demands more than saying helpful things or adopting helpful stances. It means to enjoy peace yourself, a peace which must spring from your own experience.

You may have come across people who spread a sense of relaxation round them. Tension melts when they enter a room. Matters which had us trembling or biting our fingernails suddenly seem trifles. The sun comes out when such people start to speak.

The question we must ask is not, "How do they do it?" It is not what they do that matters but what they *are*. They are themselves at peace. And because they are at peace they become sources of peace to others. We sense their inner rest and are both grateful for it and reassured by it. To be a source of peace then means to be so at peace within yourself that you are not ruffled by storms. Instead a sense of peace communicates itself to troubled people around you.

Lord, make me an instrument of your peace. Amen.

EIGHTEEN. Small Is Healthy ◊

Do not think of yourself more highly than you ought.
ROMANS 12:3

I am of small account." It is comforting to be reduced to size. I think of the time I entered Ely Cathedral, stark in its naked simplicity, yet awe-inspiring beyond words. My heart stood still before an upward sweep of towering Gothic arches, light and the beauty of space. It was good to feel small, good because something so great made being small at once fitting and uplifting. One cannot simultaneously be *puffed* up and *lifted* up.

We are never at home when we swell with importance. We may think we are having a high, but if so, it is a high never free from burdens and tensions. We may be hurt to see our real size for the first time, though in seeing it we will be delivered from the burden of having to keep our bloated image up to size.

There is something both profoundly healthy and holy about being small and reduced to silence. Nowadays we lay great stress on having a proper self-image. We rightly see that feelings of inferiority can hamper the way we live. To feel that we are no good gives us a hangdog, self-hating attitude toward life. But in seeking to correct such a state of affairs by having an "improved self-image," we usually mean a bigger and better idea of ourselves. Supposedly, we are to look in the mirror and be impressed by what we see.

Is this how God intends it? It seems to me that the real problem of having a poor self-image (or, in more old-fashioned terms, "an inferiority complex") lies in self-disgust. It really does not matter how small we are, but *how at peace we are* with ourselves. And he is at peace who has seen himself appropriately placed in the total scheme of things. The problem is not that we are small but that we are competitive and therefore displaced persons in the mad scramble for a place in life. Consequently we grow resentful of others, resentful even of God. We tread in the footsteps of Lucifer. We are children seeing who is the tallest, but we are measuring ourselves by false and shifting standards.

To know that we are small yet accepted and loved, and that we fit into the exact niche in life a loving God has carved out for us, is the most profoundly healthy thing I know. It does not inhibit boldness or assertiveness when these are called for, and it delivers us from silly, aggressive posturing and shouting. Knowing our real place in life we never need to feel threatened. Most of all we are left free to wonder at the glory and majesty of God, drinking in the living water and knowing what we are created for.

Please help me, great Father, to be at peace in my smallness and in my place within your sovereign plan. Help me to draw my self-esteem from belonging to you. Amen.

NINETEEN. The Forgiven Are to Forgive ◊

Forgive whatever grievances you may have against one another. Forgive as the Lord forgave you.
COLOSSIANS 3:13

F orgiveness does not just let things drift. This is easy to do, easier in fact than to have a terrible fight with whoever wronged you. You press your lips together, shrug your shoulders and say, "The Lord knows." But that isn't forgiveness.

Christ's forgiveness was positive, deliberate and explicit. Ours must be equally so.

Not long ago I was talking to a missionary who had been wronged by another. "Yes, I'll forgive him," the missionary said, "but things can never be the same again." Is that forgiveness? Formal, cold, from behind a closed door? Can you imagine the voice from the throne of grace saying, "Yes, I will forgive you, but from now on I can't feel the same about you"? Christ's forgiveness doesn't remember. You must have heard more than once, "Yes, I'll forgive, but I'll never forget." To forgive without forgetting is not to forgive at all. God forgets. "As far as the east is from the west, so far does he remove our transgressions from us" (Ps 103:12). "You have put all my sins behind your back" (Is 38:17). "I have swept away your offenses like a cloud" (Is 44:22). "I will remember [your] sins no more" (Jer 31:34).

When you forgive you must forget too, totally. Blot the thing out of your memory. Do so at once. Put it behind you and keep it there.

Thank you for all you have forgiven and forgotten about me, Lord. Please enable me to forgive in that same way, much as I resist it. Amen.

TWENTY. God's Purpose in Guidance ◊

Blessed are those who . . . walk in the light of your presence, O LORD.
PSALM 89:15

You must grasp two things about the nature of divine guidance. First, God has an overall goal for your life; second, God's goal is a moral goal. His plan for you has less to do with geography than with ethics. His supreme object is to make you like his Son (Rom 8:29). Whether the process of making what he wants of you involves travel, money, joy, pain or whatever is secondary. His goal is to make you holy, and the kind of guidance he will give you will reflect this.

It is precisely at this point that you may have problems. Usually when we want guidance, we have in the back of our minds some overall objective toward which we are striving. I may ask you to direct me to Smith Street, but my real object is to find a certain doctor who can cure me of cancer. Similarly I may want to know whether I should apply for job A or job B, but in the back of my mind I am really struggling with vague goals which have to do with happiness, "success" or even money.

Thus, when we ask God for guidance, we may have one goal in mind while he has another. We may not therefore be interested in the kind of guidance he has to offer.

It is not that the two *kinds* of goal (geographical and moral) are unrelated. Geography and ethics go together. Generally when I want to decide between Chicago and New York, there will be some moral aspect to my decision. Perhaps I promised to go to New York, but it will be more financially rewarding to go to Chicago. And God is less worried about whether I make a mistake about the geography than about the morality. It matters less that I wind up in the wrong city than that I make a wrong moral choice.

God does not desire to guide us magically. He wants us to know his mind. He wants us to grasp his very heart. We need minds so soaked with the content of Scripture, so imbued with biblical outlooks and principles, so sensitive to the Holy Spirit's prompting that we will know instinctively the upright step to take in any circumstance, small or great.

Therefore the most important use of Scripture in relation to guidance is that through the study of it you may become acquainted with the ways and thoughts of God. Guidance is not meant to come through the point of a pin. (Close your eyes, open your Bible at random, and stick a pin into the page. The verse you have picked is your clue for guidance.) The Bible is not a celestial ouija board.

But you will say, "Doesn't the Bible speak of visions, dreams, prophecies, voices and all sorts of special interventions?" Indeed, it does. "Do these things still happen?" Yes. And I have personally experienced some of them.

But pause to think for a moment. Many of the dramatic, "special" types of guidance were given to people (sometimes ungodly and very often headstrong) who were too set on their own ways. This can be said of Pharaoh, of Moses, of Balaam, of Peter on the rooftop, of Nebuchadnezzar, of Paul on the road to Damascus and later on a non-Macedonian course, and of many others. In other instances the guidance was of so exceptional a nature that nothing less than a vision would serve (as for Mary the mother of our Lord), or the people had so little knowledge of God that they could be reached in no other way. God has something better in mind so far as your everyday walk is concerned.

His aim is that you become his companion, that you walk together with him. He already knows all about you. Now he wants you to understand more about him. The more you understand of him, the more real the companionship will be, and the more likely you are to keep in step with him in the direction he is taking you.

Father, help me to get beyond striving to find the most beneficial circumstances. Help me to strive instead to walk in the light of your presence, and guide me as I do so. Amen.

TWENTY-ONE. The Practice of the Present ◊

Do not worry about tomorrow, for tomorrow will worry about itself. Each day has enough trouble of its own.
MATTHEW 6:34

There is a signpost labeled "Do not be anxious about tomorrow." I am, to be sure, taking the words out of their context, which has to do with anxiety about our material needs. But I am not doing violence to them. Jesus is applying a general rule about anxiety to a specific situation, and it is to the general rule I wish to call attention: "Let the day's own trouble be sufficient for the day." Nowadays we express something similar when we advise people to "live a day at a time." It is sound advice. After all we can live only a day at a time. But I prefer the way Jesus puts it.

We need this signpost if we are to learn to leap rather than struggle along an uphill road. Since the future is unknown and since we, like nature, abhor a vacuum, we fill it with imagined hopes and fears which bear little relationship to the future's true content. But fears are futile. We torture ourselves with terrors that will never come to pass, wasting agony on mere fantasy.

As Christians we are called to live primarily in the present. We are to think about today—not tomorrow, but today. Today we have duties to perform. Today we may reach out and touch God. Tomorrow has not yet arrived, but today has. There may not even be a tomorrow. But today is a gift placed in our hands, a gift we can use only if we keep ourselves from being distracted by tomorrow.

Living in the present is, however, a disciplined art that has to be learned. It can become a habit of mind only if it is practiced constantly over months, even years. Nor should it be regarded, any more than the matter of rejoicing in the Lord, as just a bit of psychological uplift. To be sure it makes good psychological sense. However, it is also a Christian duty. Christians who assume too much responsibility for the future are presumptuous. They assume the prerogatives of omnipotence and omniscience, trying to nudge the Almighty aside, bidding God make room for them on his throne. Now it is one thing to be seated with Christ in heavenly places, but it is quite another to forget which seat belongs to us and which seat belongs to the Father.

To live in the present is to acknowledge that we are creatures and that God is God. It is a discipline not just of service to us but of honor to God. We are not merely advised to learn it but commanded to do so.

Lord, it is good to be a creature, to be one who is created, subject to a greater power. I have not been made to rule the flow of time. Rather, I have been made to fit into your plans and your ways. And it is good when I do. Give me the grace then, I pray, to focus on this day you have given me and not the tomorrow over which I have no control. Amen.

TWENTY-TWO. The Family of God ◊

Everyone who has left houses or brothers or sisters or father or mother or children or fields for my sake will receive a hundred times as much and will inherit eternal life.

MATTHEW 19:29

Y ou are a member of the family of God.

You were cleansed by the same blood, regenerated by the same Spirit. You are a citizen of the same city, a slave of the same master, a reader of the same Scriptures, a worshiper of the same God. The same presence dwells silently in you as in them.

Therefore you are committed to them and they to you. They are your brothers, sisters, your fathers, mothers and children in the Lord. Whether you like or dislike them, you belong to them. You have responsibilities toward them that must be discharged in love. As long as you live on this earth, you are in their debt. Whether they have done much or little for you, Christ has done all. He demands that your indebtedness to him be transferred to your new family.

There is stability in commitment. To have to make too many choices in life renders us anxious and ill at ease. There are areas in our lives where God has taken choice away—not to enslave us, but to set us free from fussing and to liberate us to make creative choices.

We are not allowed to choose our brothers and sisters or whether we shall be committed to them or not. They belong to us and we to them. We have no control over the fact that we are to love, care and be responsible for them. We may fail to live up to our commitment and rebel against Christ. But our rebellion does not abolish the commitment. It will be there as long as life shall endure.

You are committed to *all* your new brothers and sisters. While to some you will be attracted, by others you will be repelled. With some you will discover an instant affinity. There will be a spontaneous warmth and a pleasure in their company. But others will repel you. You will find yourself avoiding them, being irritated by them or else having no feelings at all about them except boredom.

But you are not to confine yourself to the favorite few. You are committed to the freaks and oddballs of the lunatic fringe as well as to those Christians about whom you feel highly critical. You belong to people you find hard to like and people whose views you disagree with. It is all part of the privilege of belonging to God.

Sometimes, Father, it's hard to thank you for all my family in Christ. But I do. It is an evidence of your magnificent saving power that you bring such a collection into your kingdom—a collection that includes me. Amen.

TWENTY-THREE.   Sharing Christ's Suffering ◊

Through faith . . . others were tortured and refused to be released, so that they might gain a better resurrection. Some faced jeers and flogging, while still others were chained and put in prison. They were stoned; they were sawed in two; they were put to death by the sword. They went about in sheepskins and goatskins, destitute, persecuted and mistreated—the world was not worthy of them.

HEBREWS 11:33, 35-38

I n addition to avoidable and unnecessary suffering, there is true suffering for Christ. Living as we do in an age of tolerance and political freedom, we forget the risks which many Christians have run in other times and places—and which some still run today.

Historically, the crucifixion of Jesus set in motion a chain reaction of harassments, imprisonments and martyrdoms for his followers that has continued to this day. In most parts of the world for most of the past two thousand years, followers of Christ have risked imprisonment and death. The light of freedom has waxed and waned many times. Sometimes Christians have gone to their deaths by thousands and have done so singing the praises of the Lamb upon the throne. At other times they have enjoyed more liberty.

It would be foolish of us to assume that our present luxurious freedom will continue indefinitely. As the biblical influence wanes, it is likely that freedom will not continue. There are signs that the conditions necessary for tolerance and freedom in the West are already being eroded.

It is therefore important that we ask ourselves, "Am I willing to risk imprisonment and death for Christ?" Where would we stand if we had to face what Christians faced in Nazi Germany in World War 2 or more recently in China and Cuba? The invitation is subtle. No one is asked to renounce Christ—only to put him in his proper place, second to people and state. The pressure is fierce.

I believe the darkness may be descending again, and I fear that few of us are prepared for it. We belong to a long tradition of martyrdom, but we have become soft and ill-prepared. Yet Christ calls us, as he called believers in the past, to pick up our nooses daily and follow him.

I don't know, dear Lord, whether I am prepared for the dramatic choice between you and my human life. Even lesser choices may be difficult for me. But I want to follow you at any cost. Help me to choose you today, in the smaller situations, so I can prepare myself for the larger choices I may be called to make in the future. Amen.

TWENTY-FOUR. Authority Abused ◇

Submit yourselves, then, to God.
JAMES 4:7

_____

There is a tension among Christians that arises from what might be called a *high view of the church* and a *high view of Scripture*. Both have their dangers. The first emphasizes the authority of the church over the lives of God's people. Similarly a high view of Scripture emphasizes the need for Scripture to control the behavior of Christians.

Both emphases are found in Scripture. There is no tension between them there. The tension arises in the minds of leaders who try to use either church or Bible or both to *control* God's people. The authority of Scripture is never to be coercive; it does not make leaders into rulers. Church leaders are themselves under the authority of Scripture.

For all his heroism and godliness, Watchman Nee, because of his high view of the church, fell into error at this point. Writing of Christ's authority, Nee stated, "Hence you [should] recognize not only the head, Christ, but also those whom God has set in the body to represent the head. If you are at odds with them you will also be at odds with God." The danger lies in the last sentence: *"If you are at odds with them you will also be at odds with God."* As Jerram Barrs puts it in *Shepherds and Sheep*, "Nee teaches that whenever Christians disagree with their leaders, they ipso facto disagree with God." The implication of Nee's teaching has throughout history been carried further than Nee might have wanted. It is currently taught in some groups to infantilize and subjugate Christians to a form of "spiritual" and sometimes physical tyranny.

And the same tyranny is exercised by people with a high view of Scripture. In their case selfishness takes the form of mistaking what God is saying in Scripture for their particular brand of interpretation of Scripture.

Christian leaders, being human, can give place to sin and pride. They are not always aware when they are doing so. They forget that our Master's total immunity (as the Son of man) to Satanic control arose from his sinless human walk. Human leaders who make pronouncements in the name of God or of Scripture may be unaware of the power of Satan over them at that moment. At the very least they will be making carnal statements in the name of God or of Scripture, while at worst they will be meriting the same rebuke that Jesus once gave to Peter, "Get behind me, Satan!"

Lord of the church, protect me from wanting to control others by the use of your body, the church, or your Word. Free me also from the legalistic grip of those who would put me under their control; help me to submit only to you. Amen.

TWENTY-FIVE. Trusting the Chief ◊

The path of the righteous is like the first gleam of dawn, shining ever brighter till the full light of day.
PROVERBS 4:18

I was nervous. My wife was to have an operation. As I tried to think of whom I could trust to do the surgery, my misgivings multiplied until I remembered "the Chief." The Chief was my old professor of surgery whom I had known for years. I had seen him operate often. I had assisted him. For hours I had watched his deft, gloved hands confidently restore order in diseased human bodies. No crisis seemed to ruffle him; no problem baffled him.

As I thought about the Chief, my anxiety subsided. Yes, this was the person to whom I would entrust my wife's life. I could trust him because *I knew him so well.*

Do I doubt God's power? Or his concern for me? If so, I don't fully know him. Knowing him, I could never doubt his power or care. It is not more faith that I need to pray for—faith as a grain of mustard seed is enough—but to know God better.

It is time to abandon the idea that faith is a kind of leap into the dark. A leap it may be; or better, a step—followed by many more steps that become a walk and way of life. We might hesitate to take them, uncertain at first of the firmness of the ground ahead. That is what makes them steps of *faith.*

But they are not steps into the dark. As we take them, we find for ourselves that they are steps into light, which grows more and more into a perfect day.

It is astounding, Lord God, that you allow us to know you intimately—you, the infinite and eternal God. More than that, you invite us to draw nearer to you! I want to know you better. Assist my small steps of faith. Thank you. Amen.

TWENTY-SIX. New Bonds ◊

Rejoice that you participate in the sufferings of Christ, so that you may be overjoyed when his glory is revealed. . . . If you suffer as a Christian, do not be ashamed, but praise God that you bear that name.

1 PETER 4:13, 16

Whenever his followers experience hostility or hardships in order that others may see and know Christ, they are truly sharing Christ's suffering. We walk with him, and the abuse that falls on him falls also on us.

And this sharing creates new bonds. Read *Foxe's Book of Martyrs* (if you can stomach it) or Merle D'Aubigné's *History of the Reformation*, and you will be astonished at the buoyant rejoicing of persecuted Christians in former ages. Their joy amazes us. Tortures that would have reduced us to jabbering idiots left them still praising God. We cannot see ourselves showing anything like the same temerity and fortitude.

What we fail to realize is that to share Christ's sufferings is also to draw near to him. And to draw near to him, be the outward circumstances what they may, is to be filled with joy. Like Stephen as rocks battered his fragile frame, we see heaven opened and know that things are not what they appear to be. In such circumstances it becomes easier to pray for our enemies.

Christians will never go through the black night Christ passed through. That was for him alone. But we shall enjoy his nearness in those parts of his suffering in which we are privileged to share. We need have no fear of them.

The idea of suffering can be fearful. Please bring ever more strongly into my heart and mind the joy of drawing near to you, Lord, in my suffering. I bear your name. In that I rejoice. Amen.

TWENTY-SEVEN. The Power of Human Forgiveness ◊

. . . forgive your brother from your heart.
MATTHEW 18:35

Our forgiveness of others determines the day-by-day relationship between God our heavenly Father and us his children. "If you do not forgive men their sins, your Father will not forgive your sins" (Mt 6:15). As long as we remain unforgiving, our communion with our Father will be broken. We have dammed the stream that was meant to flow to us and through us.

But forgiveness will do more. It has the power to change the lives of people around us. Only because God has forgiven us can we live holy lives. Being forgiven provides a wonderful incentive to righteousness. Nothing is more deadly than to live in an atmosphere of condemnation.

When we sense other people's criticism of us, we make mistakes all the more. On the other hand, a kindly, forgiving attitude brings out the best in us.

Ever been hungry for forgiveness? If so, you will have some idea of the glorious power that is in your own hands. Around you are people whose lives could be changed by your forgiveness. They are waiting for the kindly touch of it now. Give your spouse the forgiveness he or she longs for. Seal it with a kiss, a smile, a nice meal and a bunch of flowers. Be forgiving with friends, coworkers and the children, with neighbors and with hypocritical people in church.

Your local spiritual desert will blossom like a rose, and a freshness will come to your own heart that you have not known for many a year.

Grant me the grace to forgive those who have hurt me, Lord. Allow me to bestow on them the gift of a load lightened and of acceptance advanced. Amen.

TWENTY-EIGHT. Afraid of God's Anger ◊

Then David was angry because the LORD's wrath had broken out against Uzzah. . . . David was afraid of the LORD that day.

2 SAMUEL 6:8-9

My anger often arises from impatience. My pencil breaks, I put it in the pencil sharpener, but the lead snaps off just as I get it to a fine point. The same thing happens a second time. I get mad. I am in a hurry and my patience gives way. God is never in a hurry. Broken pencils never bother him.

At other times I grow angry because I am weak and powerless. The government, the boss, the income tax authorities all get at me in ways which give me no comeback. I fuss and fume because there is nothing I can do. I honk my horn in a traffic jam because I am powerless to shift the cars that hem me in. God has no need to fuss and fume. He is never frustrated. He is almighty. There is nothing that can ever resist his will.

I have seen people angry because they are afraid. God is never afraid. I have seen people angry because they dare not speak their mind. They are scared of saying to their spouses exactly what they feel, so they kick the dog instead. God speaks his Word with no thought of fear. He has no need to vent his spleen on the innocent.

What then is God's anger? It is an implacable hostility to all that is evil. Though sometimes we read of God's wrath being "kindled," the Bible is really using a figure of speech. For God's anger is fixed. It is absolute, immutable, eternal. It is part of himself. He could not remain God and cease his irrevocable rage against evil. He is angry because he is God, just as he is love because he is God. He is angry with corrupt government, with cruelty, oppression, violence, terrorism, exploitation and all the wickedness by which human beings do evil to each other.

But he restrains the expression of his anger. He is longsuffering in judgment. And when his anger is displayed he has a serious purpose in displaying it.

But why should he make people afraid? We are foolish to suppose that fear is evil. Fear can be either good or bad according to its effect upon us. A child's fear of fire can lead to a healthy respect for its destructive powers, a respect which enables the child in later life to make wise use of fire's benefits. Without fear the child could be severely burned. It would be better for the child to be so terrified that he never made use of fire, than for him to be destroyed by fire. But it is better still that the child, through fear, learn that degree of respect which enables him to harness fire's power.

Fear, then, is a steppingstone to enrichment in our spiritual life. Without fear we are exposed to dangers of which we have little or no understanding. If through fear we learn reverence for God, our feet will be set on the road that leads to wisdom.

Mighty God, set me free from unwarranted fears, I pray. But give me a healthy fear of your anger. Through it, teach me a proper view of you—and lead me toward proper worship and true wisdom. Amen.

TWENTY-NINE. Removing Guilt ◊

Your guilt is taken away and your sin atoned for.
ISAIAH 6:7

W e all know what guilt feelings are like. They make us unhappy and anxious. Some people take baths when they feel guilty. Others bury themselves in a book, or drown their anxiety in whiskey. Children avoid their parents or sit staring at their plates during mealtime.

But let me be clear. *Guilt feelings* and *guilt* are not the same thing. No two people share the same standard. What may seem wrong to you may be approved by your neighbor, whereas things you can do with a clear conscience might bother him or her tremendously. The aim of modern psychology is to rid people of guilt *feelings*, at least of those guilt feelings that prove incapacitating. In contrast, the aim of the Bible is to teach us how we can be rid of guilt itself, and what guilt really consists of.

Both approaches have merit, but it must be obvious that the Bible's approach is incomparably more important. Sin is to guilt feelings what cancer is to pain. If a man has cancer, you will do him a great service if you relieve him of his pain. But if you take away the pain without taking away the cancer (difficult, but not impossible), you do him only a partial service. If, on the other hand, you relieve him of the pain by getting rid of his cancer, you will do him a much greater service.

But what if you could not convince the person that he in fact is a victim of cancer? None of us want to be told we have a malignancy. Happy, therefore, is the person with the moral courage to take a good look at his inner self to see whether he is inwardly diseased. The Bible makes it clear what sin is. Mark 7:21-23 says, "For from within, out of men's hearts, come evil thoughts, sexual immorality, theft, murder, adultery . . . all these evils come from inside. . . ." Sinful actions spring from sinful hearts. Romans 1:18-25 tells us that the inner attitude is one of rebellion against God, a rebellion that makes us trample intellectual honesty underfoot and perverts our every instinct. "The wrath of God is being revealed from heaven against all the ungodliness and wickedness of men who suppress the truth by their wickedness. . . . For although they knew God, they neither glorified him as God nor gave thanks to him, but their thinking became futile and their foolish hearts were darkened. Therefore God gave them over . . . to sexual impurity for the degrading of their bodies. . . ." Yes, we are diseased.

God does not merely treat our pain. He removes the disease. He not only soothes our guilty feelings, but redeems us from sin. He takes account of us as whole people and gives us a whole new existence.

My Savior and great Healer, though I should die in my sin, you have redeemed me from it, made me whole and promised me life everlasting. With my whole life I give you thanks. Amen.

THIRTY. Learning to Surf ◊

Well done, good and faithful servant. You have been faithful with a few things; I will put you in charge of many things.
MATTHEW 25:21

Recently in Waikiki I watched surfers from beginners to experts. Some balanced gracefully on long and expensive boards bigger than themselves, riding for unbelievable distances with an enviable ease and style. Others were youngsters nearer the shore with short, stubby boards, learning to body surf and to pick up the skill of selecting the right wave and the right moment to get in sync with it.

Two things were clear to me. One was that the ideal way to learn surfing is as a youngster, on small waves near the shore, with a beaten-up scrap of surfboard. The big waves come later. The second thing that became clear was that there's an exhilaration in the learning. Otherwise, why would kids and adults alike go back again and again for more? Surfers are not masochists.

It is the same in following Christ. You learn best with the little waves right in front of you. Ask God to show you which they are. Commit yourself to learning on them. If you do so, you will begin to experience the exhilaration that comes with the mastery of a new skill and with it a longing to go for bigger stuff. You will have begun to experience the joy of following him fully.

Show me the small things you want me to master, Lord. May I find joy in serving you in these ways. I await the time, your time, for larger tasks and responsibilities. May I find joy in these as well. Amen.

MONTH
SIX

ONE. The Overwhelming God ◊

And the LORD said, "I will cause all my goodness to pass in front of you, and I will proclaim my name, the LORD, in your presence. . . . But . . . you cannot see my face, for no one may see me and live."

EXODUS 33:19-20

How can a human being experience an encounter with a spirit-God who is both invisible and holy? For one thing, we cannot see spirit. For another, the sight of his perfection would kill us.

Yet God, who always is more anxious to draw near to us than we are to draw near to him, can and does reveal himself in symbolic forms. Some are simple and easily comprehended and others are complex and bewildering. Yet whatever the symbolic form (readily understood to those of us who learn about the matter afterward) or however obscure, the impact on the individuals affected by it is always overwhelming.

The French philosopher Pascal left on record the fact that he had such an experience with the Lord. Scholars are both frustrated and intrigued by his sparse details. With mathematical precision he records not only the date, but the precise times of its commencement and termination. But for the content of the encounter he leaves us one word only—"FIRE!"

Others commonly describe themselves as weeping, as experiencing an appalling loss of strength, as trembling, as experiencing a strange combination of joy and terror. When the utter holiness of God is in view, people commonly suffer from an appalling sense of their own wretchedness and of their own sin.

At other times, God grants us experiences of himself that overwhelm us with his love and joy and peace. Though our perceptions are feeble in comparison to the glorious, blazing reality which almost knocks us flat, we sense with our whole being that this love, this joy, this peace are eternal reality.

Other experiences are far more ordinary, yet the Lord is in them as well. He knows what kind of reassurance we need. Sometimes he stretches our faith by not showing himself to us at all for a while. The miracle is that he cares enough to tailor the spiritual journey of each of us in the way that we need, in order to draw us closer to himself.

Holy and eternal God, I am grateful for what you have shown me of yourself. Help me not to hide from you when your presence is overwhelming; help me not to despair when you hide yourself from me. Thank you for caring about my particular life and spiritual journey. Lead me in the way that is best for me. I praise you, and will praise you. Amen.

TWO. Today's Treasures ◊

See how the lilies of the field grow.
MATTHEW 6:28

Living in the present implies enjoying today's pleasures. If you feel no pleasures exist for you today, you may not have been keeping your eyes open. I used to collect wildflowers, those explosions of delicate beauty that the Creator flings like confetti over the hedgerows and forest floor. I never realized how many there were till I started looking. I would find a strange happiness as I searched for rare ones. A new music would begin inside me.

We are surrounded—anywhere, anytime—by little beauties. A pleasing sound, the changing skies, starlight, snow crystals, birdsong, the changing seasons. We need to form the habit of looking and seeing, of listening and hearing and of pausing to savor and enjoy.

Wildflowers may not do for you what they did for me, but there are treasures, little treasures for you too, whatever your taste may be. You will have to drop some of your cares and take time to look if you want to enjoy them.

O what is life, if, full or care
We have not time to stand and stare?

One friend wrote me, "I started a *joy* box which was a collection of . . . cartoons and letters and poems and anything that brought me back to reality." I cannot state that savoring life's little treasures is a duty. Yet it is more than a psychological self-help. (And as a psychiatrist I am deeply suspicious of mere mood manipulation.) It reveals a wholesome attitude to life.

May I today see and enjoy one object of beauty. May I enjoy one hearty laugh. May I savor one delightful flavor—and give thanks to you, O Lord. Amen.

THREE. Suffering for the Gospel ◊

Blessed are you when people insult you, persecute you and falsely say all kinds of evil against you because of me.
MATTHEW 5:11

Our plane set down in Penang, Malaysia, where our team was to conduct seminars both in Penang itself and in Kuala Lumpur. Malaysia's government is Muslim, and the object of the seminars was to equip churches for evangelism.

When we were driven from the airport to meet the Malaysian Christian leaders at one of their homes, we were immediately faced with a serious question, "Are you willing to take the risk of continuing with the seminars?"

We had arrived at a time of national emergency. Public meetings were banned and the status of meetings such as our seminars was unclear. People perceived as enemies of the regime were being arrested, and among them were some Christian leaders. At that point no one was certain where the prisoners were being held or what their fate would be. Church members were afraid.

What was the real question in the minds of those leaders who asked the question? Were they asking whether we were willing to suffer, or did they themselves have fears? Were they perhaps looking for a way of telling us that it would have been better for them if we had not come? After all, it was their country, and the risks they faced were far greater than the risks we faced ourselves. We said, "You are the ones who must make that decision. The worst that could happen to us would be a day or two of prison followed by expulsion from the country. That much we will cheerfully face. Your own fates could be much worse."

The leaders glanced at one another and smiled. They had already decided what Christ wanted them to do. "We want to go ahead," they said.

Fortunately, we experienced no difficulty. True, there was one day when police watched from their vehicles as we entered and left the building. But there were no incidents, and God greatly blessed the meetings.

Not all suffering is truly suffering for and with Christ. But some is. And this is always so when the issue is the proclamation of the gospel.

Eternal God, I pray for those who face persecution today for the sake of your gospel around the world. Bless them with strength and joy in serving you. Prepare me for the persecution I may one day face, that I might be your faithful servant also. Amen.

FOUR. Should We Collaborate with Others? ◊

They had such a sharp disagreement that they parted company.
ACTS 15:39

There is already too much hostility, too much duplication of effort and competitiveness even among the genuine followers of Jesus. Whenever we can collaborate, we should. But when is it right to do so, and when is it a mistake?

Following World War 2 a committee of the World Council of Churches decided that it would be a good idea to try to bring about close collaboration, if not organizational unity, between the Inter-Varsity Fellowship (IVF) and the Student Christian Movement

(SCM) of Great Britain.

The two movements had separated years earlier over differences both about the nature and priority of the gospel. The goals of the original student movement had subtly changed. The Christian Union in Cambridge, where the evangelical movement among students was born, pulled out of the wider movement in order to be free to pursue the original goals to which they felt God had called them. Soon after, Inter-Varsity Fellowship was formed. As a student leader I was an inheritor of that tradition and of the call to pursue those goals.

But had matters changed? Had the respective goals of the Student Christian Movement and the Inter-Varsity Fellowship begun to coincide again? Some Christians thought they had and that differences were merely differences in terminology. Others thought little had changed.

Curiously, the non-Christian onlookers saw the issues with greater clarity than the Christians involved. A group at Manchester University decided to host a debate on the motion, "That the Religions of the World Are Compatible." The SCM was invited to speak in support of the motion, and I as a representative of the Inter-Varsity Fellowship was invited to oppose it. This motion had enormous implications not only for world missions but for the ethos of our respective movements.

The student union was always crowded when debates took place. Classes were cut and feelings ran high. Our debate was no exception. Every seat was taken. Students sat on window sills, leaned against the walls, crowded around the doorway and filled the corridor outside the debating hall.

We won the debate easily. Our superior skills were not the cause. Rather the non-Christians judging the debate could see that the incompatibility of world religions is not a matter of opinion but of fact. Unintentionally, they had also laid bare the radical differences between the two Christian groups.

Though it is never easy for me to turn down a friendly invitation to collaborate, the facts were such that I had to do so. There would be no merger. The goals of the two groups were totally irreconcilable.

Working together is always preferable when possible. But we must never take our eyes off our God-given objective.

Keep my attention focused on you, Lord. In seeing you, I will see who you want me to be and what you want me to do. Amen.

FIVE. When Repentance Broke Out ◊

The law was given through Moses; grace and truth came through Jesus Christ.
JOHN 1:17

I was preaching in the Canadian Maritimes. I had seen true repentance break out more than once in public, but had never observed the phenomenon when I preached myself. It had occurred to people in the hours and days following my having preached about repentance (for God himself is bringing repentance with increasing frequency these days) on several occasions, but never during the meeting.

Curiously, I had been slated to speak about repentance on this occasion, but chose not to. The Holy Spirit had impressed me with the knowledge that people in the area were more than usually gripped with sexual sin, some as aggressors, others as victims. So instead, I took sexual sin as my theme. From the moment I began to preach I sensed an unusual power, a power which had nothing to do with me or with the way I preached. God was doing something. Yet I would not say that I exerted any emotional pressure. I would describe the atmosphere in the meeting as one of alertness, yet calm. Soon a woman on the front row began to sob, and continued to do so intermittently for the whole address, comforted by the woman beside her.

As I concluded I asked those who were in the grip of sexual sins to come to the front of the auditorium for counseling and prayer. A very large number came, crowding the area around the platform. After appealing to counselors to come forward too, I prayed aloud that God would minister by his Holy Spirit to each one as he or she needed

Then we stood together quietly in God's presence.

Very soon several people began to weep. Soon the sound of sobbing, wailing and bitter cries began to fill the auditorium. Many of the men who had come forward were trembling violently. I was filled with a sense of awe, recognizing with absolute clarity that a work of God was in progress which owed absolutely nothing to my own influence in the meeting. In many people profound repentance was taking place. The tender love of God was being manifested to sinners.

God is certainly a God of justice and of judgment. He is, after all, a holy God. But of greater importance still, his nature is one of love. He *is* love. That is, the most basic component in his holiness is that of love. We can only perceive (and even then only dimly) each attribute—of holiness and of love—in the light of the other. The more I grasp his holy abhorrence of sin, the greater will be my wonder at his love.

Several times in recent months I have cried aloud in profound perplexity and wonder, "How can you *possibly* love me?" It is at this point that worship arises, repentance begins and the deepest kind of personal and church renewal starts.

Your holiness, Lord, brings together the truth of your righteousness and the grace of your love. While your law shows me to be a sinner, your Son saves me by his self-giving sacrifice. I praise you. Amen.

SIX. Chains of Gold ◊

And my God will meet all your needs according to his glorious riches in Christ Jesus.
PHILIPPIANS 4:19

Nowhere does the Bible teach that we can please God more by eating less or wearing shoes with bigger holes. "See how the lilies of the field grow," Jesus once said. " . . . I tell you that not even Solomon in all his splendor was dressed like one of these" (Mt 6:28-29). As a matter of fact, God is delighted to give us more than we need. He is not stingy. He does not measure out his blessings parsimoniously, for there is no shortage. Space and time are crammed with all he has to offer us.

Nor is it correct to say that spiritual blessings and material blessings are governed by different laws, and that we have to be poor materially in order to be rich spiritually. This is simply not true. Poor Christians, as a class, are not more spiritually blessed than Christians who have everything. Missionaries with tiny allowances do not necessarily enjoy more heavenly riches than their well-endowed colleagues. In fact, some of the poorer missionaries are so busy trying not to feel sore about the way they have to scrimp that they have no heart left to relish heavenly joys.

The fact is that God wants our lives to turn out in the best possible way. He wants us to be filled with joy, and insofar as marriage, career or ambitions will contribute to such fullness of joy, he wants these things for us too.

God doesn't want to deprive us of earthly joys but to rescue us from *bondage* to earthly joys. It is bondage that hinders blessing. God wants to rescue us not from gold but from chains of gold.

Father, please help me to get past the things in my life, and past the lack of things; take me beyond circumstances into your joy. Amen.

SEVEN. Working Underground ◊

Then they . . . commanded them not to speak or teach at all in the name of Jesus. But Peter and John replied, "Judge for yourselves whether it is right in God's sight to obey you rather than God. For we cannot help speaking about what we have seen and heard."

ACTS 4:18-20

Many years ago I visited communist Eastern Europe. I was moved by the love among the Christians whom I met and whom I was helping with Christian literature. Part of their activity was underground because a number of Christians had been imprisoned for carrying out certain activities (baptism, for example) disapproved of by the government.

What moved me most was the courage of some of the older women who would spend their afternoons distributing Christian literature. This was, of course, forbidden. To escape detection they would get on a streetcar, quickly check the passengers with experienced eyes, distribute literature, give a brief public testimony and alight at the next stop. From time to time one would be caught and sentenced to a period in jail. The fun of the game might appeal to the cops-and-robbers instinct in us; for these women it was a serious way of life. But they used their wits to escape trouble (as we did ourselves).

Ethical problems raise their heads when the church or some of its activities are driven underground. What ought I to have done when my Christian friends asked me to arrange for them to have more literature printed for them bearing a prerevolutionary date? (I didn't, but I think I might do so now.) How are we to understand Paul's and Peter's admonitions to be obedient to civil authorities (Rom 13:1-7; 1 Pet 2:13-17)?

We must recognize then that there are certain imperatives for Christians which no earthly ruler has the right to interfere with. Blessed are Christians who have the courage to defy authority under such conditions and the wisdom to avoid getting caught.

May I show due respect to my government, Lord, for you have established it. But may I also give my allegiance to you at a higher level still—and obey you when the two conflict. Amen.

EIGHT. Lord and God ◇

Then he said to Thomas, "Put your finger here; see my hands. Reach out your hand and put it into my side. Stop doubting and believe." Thomas said to him, "My Lord and my God!"

JOHN 20:27-28

What happens when the old patterns of our lives are smashed and we are set free forever to be slaves of Jesus Christ?

For the apostle Paul there was a blinding light, a voice that spoke from heaven and choking dust in his nostrils. He knew what for years he had been trying not to know, that Jesus of Nazareth was supreme in the universe.

For Thomas there came the moment of burning shame as he heard the quiet words, "Put your fingers here. . . ." All doubts about who Jesus was were forever set at rest.

Whether through terror or shame, both men were gripped by the impression that Jesus was more than a mere man. He was Lord of creation. Paul had denied it and Thomas had doubted it, yet both now confessed with their lips what their lives continued to confess thereafter, "Lord . . ."

"My Lord and my God!" The knowledge of who Christ really is may not come to you and me so dramatically. We may not be thrown to our faces or confronted with Christ's physical presence. Yet however the Holy Spirit does it, whether he uses someone's preaching or our own reading and meditation, he must bring us to the point where we cry out with Paul and Thomas, "My Lord and my God!" And we must cry out not only from our hearts but from our minds. We must understand *why* and *how* Jesus Christ is pre-eminent.

Jesus, it is one thing to say you are Lord and God—quite another to say you are my Lord and my God. May I understand today that you are supreme in my life. Amen.

NINE. The Prayer of the Broken Heart ◊

[Hannah] was deeply distressed and prayed to the LORD, and wept bitterly.
1 SAMUEL 1:10 RSV

Does grief inhibit prayer? God invites us to share our griefs with him. Some Christians feel that only praise, worship and expressions of confidence are acceptable to God. Yet grief, pain, suffering—all are a part of life and therefore may be a part of the traffic between God and you.

"Behold, O LORD, for I am in distress," cried Jeremiah, "my soul is in tumult, my heart is wrung within me. . . . Hear how I groan; there is none to comfort me" (Lam 1:20-21 RSV). The Son of man himself sets us an example. "He took Peter, James and John along with him, and he began to be deeply distressed and troubled. 'My soul is overwhelmed with sorrow to the point of death,' he said to them. 'Stay here and keep watch.' Going a little farther, he fell to the ground and prayed" (Mk 14:33-35).

Have you never groaned or wept before God? It is not right that your silence should rebuke the tender concern of the Most High, a God who listens and watches for the griefs of his people. Therefore you must not hide your grief because of mistaken notions about being spiritual or victorious. Are you more spiritual than the Son of man? If he needed to pour out his agony to the Father, then do you suppose it would be a weakness for you to do so?

Your sorrow, however, may be more than sorrow. Is there bewilderment as well as pain? You cannot understand perhaps how God could have failed to respond in the way you expected. You are torn by confusion and have to contend with bitterness and resentment toward him.

It is astonishing that the Lord high above all, the Creator of life and of time, should pay gracious heed to our tiny resentments and frustrations. Yet he does. It constitutes no lack of reverence to confess to him how confused we feel at his failure to act like the God we thought we knew. Moreover, unless we do so, we shall never hear how he replies to our complaints.

So it is not wrong to come before God with a despairing why. It is better, much better to bring it to God than to turn it into a barrier that shuts God out.

There is no better time to approach God than when we are bewildered and hurting. Should we fail to go to him, we may become feeble and twisted, bitter useless wrecks. But if we bring him our hurts and confusion, a number of things will happen. Our faith will deepen. Our minds and spirits will expand. We will have a large capacity for living. We will become more free. Most important of all, our knowledge and appreciation of God will grow.

You are big enough, God, to handle my deep distress, my great grief or my continual questioning. You won't push me away. You want to listen and you are able to understand. Thank you. Amen.

TEN. Walking through Doors of Fear ◊

The accuser of our brothers, who accuses them before our God day and night, has been hurled down. They overcame him by the blood of the Lamb and by the word of their testimony; they did not love their lives so much as to shrink from death.

REVELATION 12:10-11

Some years ago Lorrie, my wife, and I got scared. God had laid it on my heart to expound Revelation 12:1-12 as often as I could. The passage deals with three critical ways in which the feeblest Christian can overcome Satan, and whenever I explained this, Christians were moved and profoundly helped. But I soon discovered that in preaching and writing about spiritual battles I had gotten myself and my family into our own spiritual battle.

Every time I preached on the passage something major or minor would happen to my wife or to one of the children, usually in the form of a mishap or an accident. At first I thought it must be a series of coincidences. Later it became clearer to Lorrie and to me that no coincidence was involved. Progressively the incidents became more serious. After praying about the matter, Lorrie and I felt clear about our course of action.

We knew that Satan is the "devouring dragon" and "a roaring lion." But we also knew that the only way to overcome him in that capacity was to "love not our lives even unto death." We determined, along with our children, that we would not back down. For we also had learned that the lion roars more frequently than he devours. His first aim is to intimidate us. He wants to scare us into backing down, and evidently he wanted to stop me from preaching that particular message.

The attacks continued. Some months later I was to preach in St. Helen's Church in London, England. The church was crowded with African students and others who were studying medicine in Russia and other eastern European countries, but who had come to Britain to attend a conference organized by the Christian Medical Fellowship. It was a moving occasion, powerfully used by God.

But the same night that I preached in London, Lorrie in Canada was placed in the intensive care unit of a nearby hospital with a severe coronary attack. Her life was in danger. When later the next morning I received a telephone call from my oldest son, I knew exactly what the score was and did some hard thinking.

In spite of the seriousness of Lorrie's condition, I decided to continue at the conference and to keep in touch by telephone. I was able to speak to Lorrie herself a day or two later, and we agreed that we would still not back down to pressure whatever happened.

But that was the last time we were troubled. A number of years have passed, and never again has there been an attack following my preaching of Revelation 12. I have expounded the passage again and again. Interestingly, Lorrie was divinely healed of her heart condition four years later.

The lesson has come hard, but I am learning that since it is Satan's prerogative to intimidate, it is mine to walk through doors of fear. And when I do so, it is only to discover that in most cases there has been nothing to fear. True, I fight in a real war, and there will be real casualties. But most of our fears will prove unfounded if, sure of our calling, we walk through doors of fear.

Sometimes I fear commitment, Lord. May I then, with your aid, face the door I must walk through, and take my courage in both hands. Amen.

ELEVEN. Cuckoo in the Sparrow's Nest ◊

We know that our old self was crucified with him so that the body of sin might be done away with, that we should no longer be slaves to sin.
ROMANS 6:6

S elf is like the cuckoo. Cuckoos lay their eggs in other birds' nests. A baby cuckoo in a sparrow's nest may be three times the size of its foster parents. I will never forget the comic-tragic sight of a pair of hedge sparrows, frantically darting to and from their nest to supply an enormous baby cuckoo with bits of food. It amazed me to see what power the cuckoo held to keep the sparrows on the move. His lusty cries could be heard for a quarter of a mile. The sparrows had grown thin and weary in their endless haste to cram food into his insatiable gullet.

Self is a cuckoo in the nest of your heart. Like the sparrows, you are driven mercilessly by his cries to be satisfied. And the bigger he gets, the hungrier he grows; while the hungrier he grows, the louder he shrieks.

But there's another aspect to the problem. So long as the cuckoo in the nest gets preference, the weak cries of the baby sparrows are less effective in securing food from their parents. In the same way, so long as the strident voice of self enslaves you, the real you, the redeemed you, the new creation in Christ, will have little chance to grow. You'll be too busy feeding the demands of self.

How did we get to be saddled with a cuckoo of such proportions?

Where did the monster come from?

Self is that within us which defied and still defies the sanctifying lordship of Christ. Self is that part of us that still wants to run our lives. And because self is astute, it has fooled us into believing it can give us a better deal than Christ. In fact, it is subtler still: self fools us into believing that it is us—and that we are the ones in control.

But are we? The theory holds no water, theologically or practically. After all, we are the ones being run ragged. Self is the creature crying for more food. Of course, if we submit to its cries, if we identify with it, go along with its plans, then I suppose there is a sense in which we become one with the self.

As God sees it, however, the real me is the redeemed me. What Christ redeemed included my very core, and having freed it he gave me liberty to choose whom I would serve (see Rom 6:12-14). The whole point is that before being redeemed I had no choice but to be errand boy to a cuckoo. Having been redeemed, I have the power to choose.

So notice the change. Formerly we were slaves because we couldn't help ourselves. "You who used to be slaves to sin" (Rom 6:17). Now (if Christ really has redeemed us) we are either free indeed or slaves by choice. We don't have to spend the rest of our days feeding a cuckoo, for we are under no obligation to it whatsoever!

Lord Jesus, you died to free me from everything evil, including the gluttony of self. Help me daily to claim the freedom you have given. Help me to choose to ignore self's clamoring and to live instead to please you, my redeemer. Amen.

TWELVE. The Fellowship of Pain ◊

Praise be to . . . the Father of compassion and the God of all comfort, who comforts us in all our troubles, so that we can comfort those in any trouble with the comfort we ourselves have received from God.

2 CORINTHIANS 1:3-4

P ain can separate us from others. And yet I say, *do not grieve alone.* There must be someone, somewhere with whom you can share your pain. Find that someone.

I know that you may have shared your pain with God. However, I speak of a fellow human. I agree that not everyone will want to share your burden. You may question your right to share it. Yet Christian fellowship exists, among other things, for the sharing of pain and of pleasure. Pain shared is pain divided. Pleasure shared is pleasure multiplied. Therefore Christian fellowship, where it is a true sharing-praying fellowship, can be a resource of incalculable value.

I suppose there is a sense in which our suffering contributes to the well-being of the fellowship, especially if we have been able to discover God's help in our pain. Paul blesses God who is the Comforter and who teaches us to comfort one another.

I write as one who has tasted the bitterness of despair and found a larger God as a result of groping in the darkness. Let us join as a fellowship of pain—or, better, a fellowship of people who through pain have grasped the hand of a larger, more powerful and more tender God than ever we knew existed.

Thank you, Lord, that you made us for fellowship. Yet it is so easy to let pain isolate me from those who would care for me. Break through my walls so I can experience their concern and be healed. Amen.

THIRTEEN. Praise Where Praise Is Due ◊

I do not cease to give thanks for you.
EPHESIANS 1:16 RSV

P aul is not being diplomatic but simply telling the truth. He constantly praises God for the Ephesians.

How important is it that he should do so? To give thanks for a fellow believer is important for at least two reasons.

In the first place God deserves to be praised for his creation. He has taken interest in someone who never merited it. He wooed a person with his Holy Spirit; he brought a thousand small circumstances to bear on the person's life, preparing the person to see his or her sin and the grace of God toward it. He cleansed, quickened, adopted the person as his son or daughter. He did this for countless men and women and children. But even if only one person were to exist with whom God took such pains, it would be the duty of all of us to praise and thank him for such amazing kindness.

But there is a second reason why we should give thanks. We cannot give thanks and remain the same. Our perspective changes as we open our minds to God through prayer. Hope is quickened. Is the person we pray for a difficult case? If so, are we perhaps focusing on the difficulties rather than on the God of difficulties, on what has *not* been done rather than on what *has* been done?

Begin your prayer with thanksgiving. Thank God that he reached down from heaven to seize the one for whom you pray. Thank him for any evidence, past or present, of his work. Thank him for his unchanging purposes toward the person you pray for. Only when you have done so will you begin to see things in a proper light.

Praise be to you, O God, for your creation of the world, and especially of the wonder of what human beings are. I give you thanks today for the people who are important to me. Amen.

FOURTEEN. No Wood for the Fire ◊

Without wood a fire goes out; without gossip a quarrel dies down.
PROVERBS 26:20

I f tearing others down is a temptation, how can we overcome it? First, by not listening to gossip or criticism. When we listen, we increase the gossip's sense of importance. We give him or her an audience.

This is hard advice. We may really *want* to listen. And it is embarrassing to cut someone's gossip off in midstream. But we can be tactful in the way we do it. We might say, "Look, Bob, the Lord's shown me that I have a weakness for pointing out other people's failures. He's been dealing with me about it. If you don't mind, we'd better change the subject." Make the break clean. We will have made Bob search his own conscience, and what's more, it will dawn on him someday that if we won't listen to his gossip about someone else, neither will we listen to someone else's gossip about him. He will respect us for it.

My mother had an infallible method for coping with gossips and critics. I'll never forget the day when the lady next door was dripping vitriol about the neighbor on the far side. My mother took hold of her neighbor's arm. "Come on," she said, "let's go and talk to her about it." It was the last time our next-door neighbor ever criticized another neighbor in my mother's presence.

She did the same with all the neighbors. Did she miss out on all the gossip? Well, maybe she did. I never asked her. But what she lost in back-fence gossip she gained in outpoured confidences. The women knew they could come to her with a personal problem or a heartache. They could trust her tongue. She probably had a more accurate, if less lurid, knowledge of what went on in the neighborhood.

I would like to have a trustworthy tongue, Lord. Work in me, please, to that end. Amen.

FIFTEEN. The Ultimate Test ◊

Take your son, your only son, Isaac, whom you love, and go to the region of Moriah. Sacrifice him there as a burnt offering.

GENESIS 22:2

The climax and greatest turning point of Abraham's life was the sacrifice of his promised son, Isaac (Gen 22:1-18). Nowhere else in the Bible does God command human sacrifice. Indeed the sacrifice by parents of their offspring is singled out as being abhorrent to God. Why did God command Abraham to do something he hated?

God, we read, tested Abraham. Abraham was not a twentieth-century person, but a child of a dark age where the offering of one's children to a god in sacrifice was common as the ultimate proof of love and trust. Would he trust God enough to obey the command as an act of devotion? Having waited years for the impossible—a child from his own and Sarah's bodies—could he trust God to keep the promise made at Haran, a promise repeated many times since?

Abraham's decision to sacrifice Isaac represents the last step of his journey. If we view it as a commitment, his commitment is now complete. If we view it as faith (where the true heart of the matter lies), his trust in God is great enough now to fly in the face of instinct and common sense. So much is he prepared to gamble on the word of God that he gets ready to plunge a knife into the body of his own boy, because he "reasoned that God could raise the dead" (Heb 11:19).

The knife was raised but God intervened. Abraham's bewildered eyes saw a living ram caught in a thicket beside him. His ears heard the now-familiar voice telling him to release the ropes that bound his son to the altar. God's purpose was accomplished. He had taught a human to trust him.

And this is all he wants to teach you. Whether you hear him or not, he is calling you. Tune out other clamoring sounds. In the depths of your spirit he waits to meet you.

Let there be no doubt in my mind, Lord, that you are going to extraordinary lengths to communicate with me. Indeed, you already did so when you sacrificed your son to atone for my sin and raised him to life that I might live. Amen.

SIXTEEN. The Hands of Love Reach Down ◊

He reached down from on high and took hold of me. . . .
2 SAMUEL 22:17

For many years I was frightened of being loved. I did not mind *giving* love (or what I thought was love), but I grew ill at ease if anyone—man, woman or child—showed too much affection for me. In our family we had never learned how to handle love. We were not very expert at demonstrating it or at receiving it.

I don't mean that we did not love one another or that we did not find ways of showing it. But we were very British. When I was nineteen and leaving home to go to war, my father did something quite unprecedented. He put his hands on my shoulders and kissed me. I was stunned. I knew neither what to say nor what to do. For me it was embarrassing while for my father it must have been very sad.

The matter went deeper. For years I realized intellectually that Christ loved me, but I did not want him to come too close with his love. I wanted to follow him and was willing (I think) to die for him if necessary. I loved *him*. Sometimes I could express my love to him fervently in prayer. But at the same time I was scared of his love getting too close to me.

One day I had a vision, a real one in three dimensions and full color. I was praying with friends at the time and was acutely conscious of my particular problem, my fear of being loved. Gradually I became aware that the hands of Christ were outstretched toward me a little distance away, in front of me and above me. They didn't just appear. It was as though they had been there always but that I had never really paid attention to them before. I noticed the nail prints. While I was fully aware that what I saw was a mental phenomenon, I found myself sweating profusely and trembling. Tears ran down my cheeks.

The hands were outstretched as if to invite me to take hold of them, yet my arms hung like lead by my sides. With all my heart I wanted to reach up, but I was powerless. Beneath my fear of love was a still deeper longing to be loved, to know I was loved, to receive love. The vision and my helplessness symbolized my inner problem. I wept bitterly. "O Lord, I want to grasp your hands." Over and over I repeated the words, "But I can't." Then, slowly the vision receded into the back of my mind.

In the quietness that followed, there came to me an assurance that the defensive wall I had built around me would gradually be dismantled and that I would learn what it was to let Christ's love wrap around me and fill me. And thus it has proved.

You express your love for me in many ways. Enable me to reach out in response. I am awkward, but I want to do so. Thank you, Lord Jesus. Amen.

SEVENTEEN. Getting in the Wheelbarrow ◊

And without faith it is impossible to please God, because anyone who comes to him must believe that he exists and that he rewards those who earnestly seek him.

HEBREWS 11:6

Acknowledging the strength of the evidence is only the beginning of faith. In order to believe (in the Christian sense), you do not merely assent to certain propositions. You gamble your life on those propositions. You believe that God exists? Very well, bow down at his feet. You believe he is good? Then trust him enough to do whatever he tells you. You believe he can cure the ills of your soul? Then go to him for help.

Years ago, the great acrobat Blondin, in his bid for world acclaim, had a tightrope stretched across Niagara Falls. Spellbound crowds watched him cross it, turn somersaults on it, push a wheelbarrow above the awesome plunging. The incredulity of New York newspapers turned to wondering admiration as eyewitness accounts multiplied. Blondin continued. His star was rising. Confidence in his prowess was growing.

"Do you believe I could push you across safely?" he asked one visiting celebrity.

"I do indeed," was the hearty reply.

"Then get in," said Blondin.

The celebrity declined.

Yet this is what faith is. Christian faith is to gamble your existence on the reliability of God, to "get in the wheelbarrow."

My counsel for Christians who seek such faith is: go over the evidence, one more time. You will find it as firm as ever. Read the promises of Scripture. Remember, "faith comes from . . . the word of Christ" (Rom 10:17).

Lord, going across Niagara in a wheelbarrow with you is safer than sitting in a locked bank vault without you. Thank you that faith in you is firm and sure. Amen.

EIGHTEEN. The Evidence of God's Presence ◊

But Abram said, "O sovereign LORD, how can I know that I will gain possession of it?" So the LORD said to him, "Bring me a heifer, a goat and a ram, each three years old, along with a dove and a young pigeon."
GENESIS 15:8-9

Y ears before the climactic scene by the altar, God had spoken to Abraham in terms that Abraham could not possibly have mistaken.

The local custom in making a contract called for an unusual ceremony. An animal would be divided in half and the two halves laid a few feet apart. Parties to the contract would walk between the divided remains of the animal. In doing so they were saying by the symbol, "May my body be cut in half, in the way this animal's body is, if I should betray my word and break my covenant." Such a contract was exceedingly solemn and binding.

Even before Abram's name was changed to Abraham, God made exactly this sort of covenant with him. Abram was instructed to take five living creatures (signifying the extreme solemnity of the occasion)—a heifer, a female goat, a ram, a dove and a pigeon—and to divide the animals (the heifer, the goat and the ram) in half, laying them out according to the prescribed covenant ritual (Gen 15:1-10).

At the time Abram had grave doubts about God's promise to him. His faith was low. Nevertheless, he laid out the animals in the accepted manner and waited. Hours passed. Vultures descended from time to time to seize the dead flesh, and Abram was obliged constantly to drive them away. Slowly the sun went down, and as it did so a nightmare-like trance passed over Abram. Further revelations of God's will were made to him. Then, in the darkness a glowing brazier and a flaming torch appeared, symbolizing the presence of God. Both the brazier and the torch passed between the divided halves of the dead animals. "To your descendants," the voice came, "I give this land" (Gen 15:11-21). The whole incident constituted a seal that any nomad of that age would understand.

You say you wish God would go to such pains to speak to you? Stand at Golgotha as the horror of darkness falls. Look at the God-man who hangs in extremity from a gallows. Dare you demand further evidence of God's good will in his negotiations with you? The brazier and the torch have passed between the animals. God has committed himself. He has spoken the irrevocable word for your comfort and your assurance.

Forgive me for doubting that you are speaking to me, Lord. Give me ears to hear and a will to heed your voice. Amen.

NINETEEN.   The Right to Rule ◊

Through the Spirit of holiness [Christ Jesus] was declared with power to be the Son of God by his resurrection from the dead.

ROMANS 1:4

J esus Christ has the right to rule in every area of our lives because he has conquered sin and death. In these realms earthly-governments are powerless.

The best the government and the police can do is to try to keep evil in check, just as individuals can try to control their own evil bent. But unless we have help from the outside, we are powerless in the hands of sin and death, our real masters. Where is the governor or the individual who is not subject to sin and death? Yet Jesus Christ has judged sin and death. He has been declared the Son of God with power by rising from the dead.

Jesus Christ has the right to rule in every area of our lives because he has overcome our previous masters by humbling himself to a death of public ignominy. Many earthly rulers pretend to humble themselves. Candidates for office often boast of their working-class origin or see to it that the press publishes pictures of them shaking hands with poor people. Why? Because it is recognized that those who rule must have firsthand experience of the problems of those they rule over. Jesus qualifies.

No one has humbled himself so completely as Christ, who hid his glory from our view. He came to earth and became not only a human being but a member of a working-class home. Christ knew hunger, criticism, weakness and loneliness, and he ended up pilloried to a shameful gibbet as if a common criminal. He became identified with the people he came to govern. In return for his suffering, God "exalted him to the highest place and gave him the name that is above every name, that at the name of Jesus every knee should bow" (Phil 2:9-10).

O exalted Lord Christ, I too bow before your majesty and thank you for your humiliation. You became poor and despised so that I might be made rich and enter into glory. I cannot properly thank you, Lord. Accept my small attempt. Amen.

TWENTY . Lord of History ◊

God placed all things under [Christ's] feet.
EPHESIANS 1:22

J esus Christ is the Lord of history, actively involved in the world's politics. He is cognizant of tomorrow's revolutions in Africa and Latin America. He has his hand on the stock exchange and U. S. presidential elections. As Lord, Jesus Christ knows the name of the next Russian premier and is supreme in every decision made.

The Scriptures declare, in 1 Corinthians 15:27, that God has put all things under Christ's feet, in subjection to him. What do "all things" include? All the things that God has controlled from the dawn of history. He has control over the affairs of earthly rulers. "The king's heart is a stream of water in the hand of the LORD; he turns it wherever he will" (Prov 21:1 RSV). Christ shares in this ruling supremacy.

Many find it difficult to believe that Jesus Christ is writing history. But running the world is not our job. It is his responsibility. And we may rest in the ability of his powerful hands, once pierced for our sins.

Lord of history, I confess I sometimes find it hard to see your hand in the awful events suffered daily by nations and individuals on this earth. But I ask you to continue your sovereign care over all things, and to deliver suffering people from their suffering, and to punish those who inflict suffering, and to bring about peace and justice across this planet. Apart from you we have no hope. Amen.

TWENTY-ONE. Lord of Knowledge ◊

You will know the truth, and the truth will set you free.
JOHN 8:32

J esus is the Lord of all knowledge. He has the final answers to the deepest questions people have ever asked. Does life have meaning? Why are we here? Why do we suffer? Is there a God? What is he like?

Scientists cannot answer these questions because God cannot be analyzed in a test tube or under a microscope. His handiwork can be examined, but this will not give final answers. The greatest of philosophers have long realized what scientists are now discovering—if we rely only on our own minds and observations, we can never know if God exists, and if he exists, what he is like. "Can you fathom the mysteries of God?" asked Zophar (Job 11:7). "Can you probe the limits of the Almighty?" The answer is clear. Not just by searching into what he has made.

But thank God we do not have to rely on our own powers of investigation. A voice has spoken from the silence. Christ entered history. If men and women let him, Christ can illumine their minds. No one can have true knowledge apart from him. He is "the true light that gives light to every man" (Jn 1:9).

Our relationship with Jesus determines the extent to which he will enlighten our minds. If our minds are to glow with understanding, they need to be quickened with life. They need to be controlled by the Lifegiver. We must allow him to control our logic; we must bring our thoughts into captivity to him (2 Cor 10:5). In doing so we will know the truth, and the truth will make us free.

Lord, freedom is not doing what I want but doing what you made me for. Give me the freedom to do your will. Amen.

TWENTY-TWO. Lord of the Little Things ◊

Whoever can be trusted with very little can also be trusted with much.
LUKE 16:10

C hrist is Lord of the little things in our lives too. For the little things are more important than the big. He must be the sovereign in all our affairs. In Luke 16, Jesus is teaching that the person who is faithful in a very little (that is, in money matters) will be faithful about the greater affairs of God's kingdom.

The question we must ask is, Was he the Lord of our behavior at breakfast this morning? Was he the Lord of our lips when supper burned? Is he the Lord over the resentment we cherish against others? The answer must be, Yes, he is. Jesus Christ is Lord. If we disobey him in small things, we are rebels. Someday thrones and dominions will fall at the feet of Jesus, but we are not to wait until then. We are to worship him now. We must make him absolute Lord of the next sixty seconds, and then of all the little things we do in the next five minutes. We must make a new way of life that starts at once. We must be worthy of our worthy Lord.

"Worthy is the Lamb, who was slain, to receive power and wealth and wisdom and strength and honor and glory and praise!" (Rev 5:12). Amen!

Lord Christ, you are mighty and exalted. The little things of my life seem unrelated to that. But since you are Lord of everything, help me to make my minutes, my thoughts, my small actions such that they will please you and bring glory to you. Thank you that there is nothing too small for your Lordship to include. Amen.

TWENTY-THREE. Wait and Worship ◊

I will stand at my watch and station myself on the ramparts; I will look to see what [the LORD] will say to me.

HABAKKUK 2:1

P erhaps you are waiting for God. Perhaps he seems silent, inactive or inattentive.

Go to the Scriptures. Read in the Gospels all that took place. Spend time meditating, letting the Holy Spirit speak to you from the passages. Christ's body was of human flesh and it was lifted up on a cross. The darkness actually descended. The veil in the temple was torn in two. These things happened and were recorded that you might know God has committed himself to anyone who trusts him.

He has gone to great pains to assure you that the gamble of faith is no gamble; that your commitment, your sacrifice, your step of faith will represent an entry into a deeper relationship with himself. The cost to you is trivial. What he offers is of far greater value. But you must believe—enough to take some specific step.

If you are uncertain, be in no hurry to decide what that step is. Do not move in fevered panic. Wait before God in silence. Are there pressures and frustrations? Go to the tabernacle within yourself where God abides in stillness. Tell him you want to worship him.

He will speak since he is more anxious to reach you than you are to be reached. He is in fact already speaking. It is only necessary that you learn to listen.

Lord of my years, Lord of history, Lord of all eternity, thank you that you speak to your people. Sometimes my problems are so loud that they drown out your voice. Make me quiet inside so I can hear you speak. Focus my mind so I can see your acts of love on my behalf two thousand years ago—and today. Amen.

TWENTY-FOUR. Rejoice Is a Verb ◊

We also rejoice in our sufferings, because we know that suffering produces perseverance; perseverance, character; and character, hope.
ROMANS 5:3

We rejoice. This is not to say that we experience spontaneous feelings of pleasure. We are not called to be masochists. "No discipline seems pleasant at the time, but painful" (Heb 12:11). *Rejoice* is a verb. It means to adopt a specific attitude. *Happiness* and *pleasure* are nouns. We can't *happy*. But we can rejoice. How?

We can deliberately recognize the fact that God knows what is happening to us, that he is not trying to be mean (no good parent enjoys having to give small children their swats) and that he has a plan behind the experience, a plan for our well-being. We can and should deliberately thank him, not for the suffering itself, but for his faithful control of it and his blessed purpose in allowing it. Our confidence in him at this point will actually halve the pain, and may even make it negligible.

And what is the purpose behind suffering? ". . . suffering produces perseverance. . . ." Spontaneous faith, faith on the spur of the moment, is useful. What is more necessary for a true disciple of Jesus, however, is steadfast, unwavering faith, faith that holds on when times are tough. Such *enduring* faith can develop in only one way, and that is through suffering.

Lord, you know I shrink from suffering. Unless you teach me how to be thankful in the midst of it, and how to rejoice, I never shall be able. Trembling, I ask you to do so. In Jesus' name, Amen.

TWENTY-FIVE. The Cosmic Battle ◊

I saw heaven standing open and there before me was a white horse, whose rider is called Faithful and True. With justice he judges and makes war. His eyes are like blazing fire, and on his head are many crowns. . . . He is dressed in a robe dipped in blood, and his name is the Word of God. The armies of heaven were following him.

REVELATION 19:11-14

The warfare on earth, as terrible and widespread as it is, is merely part of a larger cosmic warfare. Nowhere is its climax portrayed more vividly than in the nineteenth and twentieth chapters of Revelation. In blood-dipped clothing the King of kings rides a white charger. He is about to conquer the world in a horrifying battle, when he will tread down "the winepress of the fury of the wrath of God Almighty" (Rev 19:15).

Coming against him are the armies of the world led by the Beast and the False Prophet. The Beast seems to symbolize the tyranny and the godlessness of human government. The False Prophet represents false religion, always the ally of corrupt government. He has helped to entrench the power of the Beast by performing miracles and signs that have deceived the people. Both Beast and Prophet are captured in the battle and flung into the lake of fire.

We must notice two things about the scenario. John is giving us the obverse side of earthbound political structures. Human government is at once the God-given means by which lawlessness is held in check and that mechanism of rebellion by which we supplant God's government. In Romans 13 Paul sees government as God's sovereign kindness to us. In Revelation John sees it as our alliance with the prince of this world.

We think of most modern governments as secular. The secularism is illusion, as is the politicized charade of religion enacted by some western political leaders. No country in the world is immune from the danger of being governed by the Beast and the False Prophet, and Christians in the West are in grave danger of being fooled by them. It is power that interests most political leaders. And Satan has it to offer. Throughout history kings, emperors and presidents have been eager to acquire it from whatever source. Beast and False Prophet are once more cheek by jowl. So the battle, the battle by which the King of kings finally establishes unopposed rule, is already in progress. It is a battle that has ebbed and flowed for centuries. Its tempo is now quickening. May we be ready for the King's return.

Mighty King, you are powerful, you are victorious. You will deal with all evil. Reign forever, King of kings! Amen.

TWENTY-SIX. Two-Edged Sword ◊

No discipline seems pleasant at the time, but painful. Later on, however, it produces a harvest of righteousness and peace for those who have been trained by it.

HEBREWS 12:11

There are two sides to pain. It has as much potential for character destruction as for character building. The pain that makes robust saints can equally well create embittered, defeated cynics. Everything depends on the sufferer's response.

Before plastic surgery became technically sophisticated, a famous film star damaged her lovely face in a car accident. The surgeon explained that the damage could be repaired and her beauty restored but that the operation would have to be carried out (for certain technical reasons) without any anesthetic. She had to choose between excruciating pain and her career on the one hand or no pain and no career on the other. She chose pain.

During the operation the actress's cooperation was vital. It meant remaining perfectly still during moments of extreme suffering. When a scalpel was carefully shaping a rounded curve of skin, a sudden move of her head would have increased the damage. In actual fact the reconstruction of a beautiful face was accomplished by collaboration between the surgeon and the actress.

It is much the same in the Christian life. The pain we suffer does not produce automatic results. As the writer to the Hebrews puts it, "Later on . . . it produces a harvest of righteousness and peace *for those who have been trained by it*" (Heb 12:11). Those who have not been trained by pain are usually damaged by it. To be trained by it means to have adopted a believing, rejoicing, thankful attitude whenever one meets frustration, pain or even what from a human perspective would be viewed as tragedy and catastrophe.

The range of its forms and of its severity is infinite. My wife spilled blueberries all over a pale green carpet while I was in the middle of the previous sentence. Cars that won't start or that stall in the middle of an intersection—and a thousand petty annoyances as well as indescribable horrors—are included. All come by God's sovereign purpose. The results depend on the ways we habitually respond.

Pain terrifies me, Lord; I confess I want to run from it. I can accept it, can rejoice in the midst of it, can be thankful for its benefits, only with your supernatural help. Please train my soul to respond rightly to what my body or emotions may have to endure. I want to feel your peace; I want to mirror your holiness. Amen.

TWENTY-SEVEN. God's Temple ◊

I will put my Spirit in you and you will live.
EZEKIEL 37:14

In the Old Testament the Holy Spirit is described as dwelling in certain people. Some scholars deny this. But Peter seems quite clear on the matter, referring to the way in which "the prophets . . . searched intently . . . trying to find out the time and circumstances to which the Spirit of Christ in them was pointing" (1 Pet 1:10-11).

Pharaoh referred to Joseph as "one in whom is the spirit of God" (Gen 41:38). Not being a follower of the true God he might not have known what he was talking about. But God told Moses about Bezalel,

"See, I have chosen Bezalel son of Uri, the son of Hur, of the tribe of Judah, and I have filled him with the spirit of God" (Ex 31:2). God later said to Moses, "Take Joshua son of Nun, a man in whom is the spirit" (Num 27:18). David asked God not to remove the Holy Spirit from him (Ps 51:11).

But the indwelling of the Spirit in the Old Testament was only an exceptional anticipation of a more general blessing to be realized in the New. That is what Ezekiel referred to when he prophesied, "And I will put my Spirit in you and move you to follow my decrees" (Ezek 36:27).

For in the New Testament the indwelling Spirit was to give all believers the authority to be called sons and daughters of the living God, sanctifying, guiding and instructing them as they were given a new life that took the fear of death and mortality away.

All believers, from the moment of their conversion, are indwelt in this way. The indwelling both defines the status of believers and gives them immortality. As Paul puts it, "If anyone does not have the Spirit of Christ, he does not belong to Christ. . . . And if the Spirit of him who raised Jesus from the dead is living in you, he who raised Christ from the dead will also give life to your mortal bodies through his Spirit, who lives in you" (Rom 8:9-11). In this sense all of us are jointly and individually God's temple (1 Cor 3:16).

Spirit of God, thank you for indwelling my life and working in and through it. Help me not to grieve you but to cooperate with your wonderful purposes, so that the mighty Triune God may be both pleased and honored. Amen.

TWENTY-EIGHT. My Naked Spirit ◊

Father, into your hands I commit my spirit.
LUKE 23:46

Y ou will die only once and therefore you will have only one chance of dying properly. There will be no rehearsals for most of us. Learn your lines well beforehand so that the curtain falls on a note of triumph.

At the time of death a person becomes aware that in a moment there will be no clothing for his spirit. Stark naked it will face the fiery, icy blasts of eternity with no body to shelter it. A man whose clothes are torn from him does not think about whether he will ever get his jacket back but about how he can face life so uncovered. It is his nakedness that discomforts him.

Oh, how shall I, whose native sphere
Is dark, whose mind is dim,
Before th' Ineffable appear,
And on my naked spirit bear
The uncreated beam?

In the light of such fears the words of Jesus make sense: "Into your hands I commit my spirit." He does not say, "Into your hands I commit my *body*." It is in the *spirit* alone that he will storm the gates of hell to declare his triumph over death and sin. Spirit and body are temporarily to be separated and what he faces is the sudden stripping away of that body from the personal spirit of Jesus the man. (For Jesus was not merely God inside a body. While remaining God, he *became* man, assuming not only man's outward form but his inward personality.)

When you face death, then, it is this that you will face, not the dissolution of your body, but its being stripped (for repair and renewal) from your spirit.

Do not let the nakedness make you afraid. The God who breathed into your nostrils the breath of life, who also redeemed you and plans to clothe you with immortality, will be there in the wings to receive you personally. The curtain may fall and your bodily costume be taken (temporarily) from you, but you can walk with confidence toward your Maker and Redeemer saying in triumph, "Here is my spirit. Take it, it is yours. Clothe it again when you are ready. Into your arms I gladly bring it."

Thank you that you are Lord of both my spirit and my body. I entrust both to your care and look forward to eternal wholeness. Amen.

TWENTY-NINE. Your Closing Lines ◊

Our God is a God who saves; from the Sovereign LORD comes escape from death.

PSALM 68:20

John Donne, metaphysical poet and Dean of St. Paul's Cathedral, London, whose seventeenth-century English still affects our everyday speech with such well-known phrases as "for whom the bell tolls" and "no man is an island," is best known for his own extraordinary valor in the face of death.

Shortly before his death, he got out of bed to preach in St. Paul's his last sermon, and what was at the time generally agreed to be his own funeral sermon, entitled "Death's Duel." His chosen text was Psalm 68:20. Returning to bed, he composed the following hymn as he died:

> Since I am coming to that holy room,
> Where, with Thy choir of saints, for evermore
> I shall be made thy music, as I come
> I tune my instrument here at the door,
> And, what I must do then, think here before.
> Since my physicians by their loves are grown
> Cosmographers; and I their map, who lie
> Flat on this bed—

So, in His purple wrapt, receive me Lord!
By these His thorns, give me His other crown
And, as to other souls I preached Thy word,
Be this my text, my sermon to mine own,
"That He may raise; therefore the Lord throws down."

Izaak Walton, Donne's biographer, writes, "In the last hour of his last day . . . his soul, having, I verily believe, some revelation of the beatific vision, he said, 'I were miserable if I might not die'; and after those words, closed many periods of his faint breath by saying often, 'Thy kingdom come, Thy will be done.' . . . Seeing heaven by that illumination . . . he closed his own eyes, and then disposed his hands and body into such a posture, as required not the least alteration by those who came to shroud him."

The play has been running a long time. You are the successor of a highly distinguished cast. The Father with the whole of the cast awaits you in the wings. Therefore let the words ring out so that they reach the furthest corners of the theater, "Father, into your hands I commit my spirit." They will form the last prayer you utter on earth.

They will be your closing lines in Act I.

Eternal God, I am very fond of living in earthly time. I know you have something far better for me; I want to please you by the way I cross over, when the moment comes. Work in my spirit to that end, I pray. Amen.

THIRTY. Greater Than Riches ◊

By faith Moses . . . regarded disgrace for the sake of Christ as of greater value than the treasures of Egypt, because he was looking ahead to his reward.

HEBREWS 11:24-26

Both in his years of exile and later as leader of Israel, Moses learned that there is something greater than human success, greater than the comforts of life, greater than the treasures of Egypt. He saw that in the presence and purposes of the Lord is life's true treasure.

This great truth applies, of course, both in our daily lives and also in the eternity we are promised with God in heaven.

In Hebrews 11, Moses is cited as counting "disgrace for the sake of Christ" as a precious thing because of what it would bring. He knew that the world's riches, by contrast, are very temporary.

Then, in Exodus 32, we see him pleading with God on behalf of the rebellious and sinful Israelites.

Our faith rests upon the unchanging character of God as revealed by his acts in human history. And the heart of God is gladdened as he listens to Moses. He has found yet another human being who refuses to accept him as less than the God who revealed himself in history.

Moses' prayer is beautiful and moving. He freely admits the horrendous sin of his people. "Oh, what a great sin these people have committed! They have made themselves gods of gold." False riches.

Yet Moses' prayer is not one of criticism or condemnation. He is simply laying the cards on the table. He is desperate. He is too keenly aware of God's all-seeing eyes to do anything less. He also is aware that God has the right to do whatever he pleases, yet he pleads, "But now, please forgive their sin—."

Then comes the acid proof of a true intercessor. "—but if not, then blot me out of the book you have written." *Moses will stand or fall with his people.* He will live to lead them or die with them in the desert.

It might have been a discreet time to ask for a retirement party and consolidate his assets in a comfortable setting some distance from the crowd. But the Moses of Exodus and Hebrews knew that it was in following the eternal purposes of God that he would find a life far greater than riches.

And so will we.

God of history, you taught your servant Moses where true wealth lies. I sometimes find more temporal comforts appealing and do not wish to endure hardship, disgrace or deprivation for your sake. Help me to get my values straight, I pray, so that I may find favor in your sight and be useful in the ongoing work of your kingdom. Amen.

Acknowledgments

Selections in this book are taken from the following publications (originally published by IVP in the USA and Great Britain unless otherwise stated):

Daring to Draw Near, © 1977 by InterVarsity Christian Fellowship of the United States of America. Published in Great Britain under the title *People in Prayer*.

Excellence in Leadership, © 1986 by InterVarsity Christian Fellowship of the United States of America.

The Golden Cow, © 1979 by InterVarsity Christian Fellowship of the United States of America. Revised edition © 1992 by John White.

Healing the Wounded, © 1985 by InterVarsity Christian Fellowship of the United States of America.

The Masks of Melancholy, © 1982 by InterVarsity Christian Fellowship of the United States of America.

Magnificent Obsession, © 1976 by InterVarsity Christian Fellowship of the United States of America. Revised edition © 1990 by John White. Published in Great Britain under the title *Bound for Life*.

Parents in Pain, © 1979 by InterVarsity Christian Fellowship of the United States of America.

Putting the Soul Back in Psychology, © 1987 by John White. (Published in the USA only.)

The Race, © 1984 by InterVarsity Christian Fellowship of the United States of America.

When the Spirit Comes with Power, © 1988 by John White. Published in Great Britain by Hodder and Stoughton Ltd. and used by permission.

Month One

1 *Daring to Draw Near*, pages 103, 108-9/*People in Prayer*, pages 101, 106-7
2 *Magnificent Obsession/Bound for Life*, pages 15-17
3 *Healing the Wounded*, page 17
4 *The Golden Cow*, pages 9-11
5 *Excellence in Leadership*, pages 28-30
6 *When the Spirit Comes with Power*, pages 34-37
7 *The Masks of Melancholy*, pages 21-24
8 *The Masks of Melancholy*, pages 27-29
9 *Parents in Pain*, pages 28-29
10 *Putting the Soul Back in Psychology*, pages 22-23
11 *Putting the Soul Back in Psychology*, pages 75-76
12 *The Race*, pages 19-20
13 *The Fight*, pages 61-62
14 *Magnificent Obsession*, pages 31-32/*Bound for Life*, pages 33-34
15 *Daring to Draw Near*, pages 16-17/*People in Prayer*, pages 14-15
16 *The Golden Cow*, pages 54-55
17 *The Race*, pages 20-22
18 *Excellence in Leadership*, pages 57-59
19 *Healing the Wounded*, pages 27-28
20 *Magnificent Obsession*, pages 20-21/*Bound for Life*, pages 21-22
21 *Putting the Soul Back in Psychology*, pages 25-26
22 *Parents in Pain*, pages 46-47
23 *When the Spirit Comes with Power*, pages 48-50
24 *The Fight*, page 79
25 *Magnificent Obsession*, pages 32-33/*Bound for Life*, pages 34-35
26 *Daring to Draw Near*, pages 33-34/*People in Prayer*, pages 31-32
27 *The Golden Cow*, pages 92-93
28 *The Race*, pages 23-24
29 *Excellence in Leadership*, pages 59-60
30 *The Race*, pages 140-41

Month Two

1 *Magnificent Obsession*, pages 23-24/*Bound for Life*, pages 24-25
2 *The Masks of Melancholy*, pages 57-60
3 *The Race*, pages 144-45
4 *Putting the Soul Back in Psychology*, pages 47-48
5 *The Fight*, pages 81-82
6 *Parents in Pain*, pages 50-52
7 *When the Spirit Comes with Power*, pages 50-53
8 *Magnificent Obsession*, pages 37-38/*Bound for Life*, pages 39-40
9 *The Golden Cow*, pages 152-53
10 *The Race*, pages 26-27
11 *Healing the Wounded*, pages 46-47
12 *Magnificent Obsession*, pages 27-28/*Bound for Life*, pages 28-29
13 *Magnificent Obsession*, pages 28-30/*Bound for Life*, pages 29-31
14 *The Race*, page 151
15 *The Race*, pages 142-43
16 *When the Spirit Comes with Power*, pages 86-88
17 *The Fight*, pages 102-3
18 *Excellence in Leadership*, page 19
19 *Daring to Draw Near*, pages 51-52/*People in Prayer*, pages 49-50
20 *The Golden Cow*, pages 171-72
21 *The Race*, page 32
22 *Excellence in Leadership*, pages 93-94
23 *Healing the Wounded*, pages 55-56
24 *The Masks of Melancholy*, pages 77-78, 202
25 *Magnificent Obsession*, pages 34-35/*Bound for Life*, pages 35-37
26 *The Race*, pages 151-52
27 *Parents in Pain*, pages 95-96
28 *When the Spirit Comes with Power*, pages 120-24
29 *The Fight*, pages 124-25
30 *The Race*, page 49

Month Three

1 *Daring to Draw Near*, pages 58-60/
   People in Prayer, pages 56-58
2 *The Race*, pages 35-36
3 *The Race*, pages 36-37
4 *Parents in Pain*, pages 233-35
5 *Magnificent Obsession*, pages 38-39/
   Bound for Life, pages 40-41
6 *The Race*, pages 154-55
7 *Putting the Soul Back in Psychology*,
   pages 79-80
8 *Parents in Pain*, pages 98-99
9 *Parents in Pain*, pages 231-32
10 *The Fight*, pages 126-27
11 *The Race*, pages 139-40
12 *When the Spirit Comes with Power*,
   pages 141-42, 145
13 *The Race*, pages 125-26
14 *Parents in Pain*, page 100
15 *Magnificent Obsession*, pages 42-43/
   Bound for Life, pages 45-46
16 *Daring to Draw Near*, pages 92-93/
   People in Prayer, pages 90-91
17 *The Race*, pages 37-39
18 *Healing the Wounded*, pages 77-78
19 *Healing the Wounded*, pages 79-80
20 *Parents in Pain*, pages 229-30
21 *Magnificent Obsession*, pages 43-44/
   Bound for Life, pages 46-47
22 *The Race*, page 156
23 *Parents in Pain*, pages 102-3
24 *When the Spirit Comes with Power*,
   pages 226-27
25 *When the Spirit Comes with Power*,
   pages 227-28
26 *The Race*, page 192
27 *Daring to Draw Near*, pages 97-99/
   People in Prayer, pages 95-97
28 *The Race*, pages 53-54
29 *Healing the Wounded*, pages 83-84
30 *Parents in Pain*, pages 228-29

Month Four

1 *The Race*, pages 131-32
2 *Healing the Wounded*, pages 84-85
3 *Magnificent Obsession*, pages 44-45/
   Bound for Life, pages 48-49
4 *Excellence in Leadership*, pages 20-21
5 *The Fight*, pages 145-47
6 *When the Spirit Comes with Power*,
   pages 228-29
7 *Daring to Draw Near*, pages 100-
   101/*People in Prayer*, pages 90-99
8 *Parents in Pain*, pages 156-57
9 *The Race*, page 157
10 *Magnificent Obsession*, pages 47-48/
   Bound for Life, pages 51-52
11 *The Masks of Melancholy*, pages
   192-93
12 *Healing the Wounded*, pages 100-
   101
13 *The Race*, page 54
14 *Daring to Draw Near*, pages 102-3/
   People in Prayer, pages 100-101
15 *Healing the Wounded*, pages 167-68
16 *Parents in Pain*, pages 216-17
17 *The Race*, pages 64-65
18 *Magnificent Obsession*, pages 84-85,
   90/*Bound for Life*, pages 89-90, 96
19 *Magnificent Obsession*, pages 93-94/
   Bound for Life, pages 99-100
20 *The Race*, pages 136-37
21 *Excellence in Leadership*, pages 26-28
22 *The Race*, page 75
23 *The Masks of Melancholy*, pages
   203-4
24 *When the Spirit Comes with Power*,
   pages 229-30
25 *The Race*, pages 79-81
26 *Parents in Pain*, pages 220-21
27 *Healing the Wounded*, pages 181-83
28 *The Race*, page 92
29 *The Race*, page 139
30 *Magnificent Obsession*, page 89/
   Bound for Life, page 95

Month Five

1 *The Fight*, pages 174-75
2 *The Race*, page 133
3 *Healing the Wounded*, page 201